WITHDRAWN

Making School by Hand

Making School by Hand

Developing a Meaning-Centered Curriculum from Everyday Life

Mary Kenner Glover
Awakening Seed School, Tempe, Arizona

National Council of Teachers of English
1111 W. Kenyon Road, Urbana, Illinois 61801-1096

Manuscript Editor: Kurt Austin
Production Editor: Rona S. Smith
Interior and Cover Design: Doug Burnett
Cover Photo: Thompson McClellan
Cover Art: Mary Kenner Glover

NCTE Stock Number: 30372-3050

Library of Congress Cataloging-in-Publication Data

Glover, Mary Kenner.
    Making school by hand : developing a meaning-centered curricu-
lum from everyday life / Mary Kenner Glover.
        p.   cm.
    Includes bibliographical references (p.   ).
    ISBN 0-8141-3037-2
        1. Education, Elementary—Arizona—Tempe—Curricula—Case
studies. 2. Active learning—Arizona—Tempe—Case studies.
3. Interdisciplinary approach in education—Arizona—Tempe—Case
studies. 4. Elementary school teaching—Arizona—Tempe—Case
studies. 5. Glover, Mary Kenner. I. Title.
LB1563.T45G56 1997
372.19—dc20   96-39059
                                                           CIP

for Caitlin Elizabeth,
who left behind her quilt
and a lifetime of memories

Contents

Foreword

We might not give it much thought, but we who teach involve our students in a particular way of living and experiencing reality. In *Making School by Hand*, Mary Glover and the children invite us to join their learning community, to be insiders, so that we can give serious thought to their way of living and learning. Mary's book is remarkable because she tells us what she is thinking, gives us a close look at the choices she makes, and weaves throughout the text the philosophical beliefs that guide her. As insiders we observe Mary and the children at work, hear their voices, and catch a glimpse of what it is that they make. *Making School by Hand* is truly a thought-provoking book.

Children in Mary's learning community are not stuck with studying a bloodless curriculum packaged in textbooks and workbooks. Digesting ideas someone else has chewed on is not the way they learn about their world. Mary and her children examine real life, and they make their curriculum from scratch with their own hands. The children's commitments and concerns determine what will be investigated. Community issues, events, and problems are approached from perspectives that respond to the children's interests. Topics span a broad range, from head lice to AIDS to civil rights to the human body.

Problems connected to teaching a life curriculum are not limited merely to outfitting children with necessary materials. Those children who can immerse themselves in study have worked out how to make up ideas and develop their own questions. Nurturing such intellectual competence calls for teaching that fosters not only critical abilities but also the desire to question, create order, and be steadfast in the face of difficulty. Mary sorts out the complexity of this way of teaching-learning. Her book brings to life the dynamics of how she works with children's ideas and assists them in taking charge of their learning.

The quilts Mary makes are layered, and so is the text of her book. Importance of community, the place within which values are established, is a layer extending throughout the text. It is inspiring to see how the fellowship shared by children finds expression in learning and caring. The learning community that Mary makes with her children prizes making a deliberate effort to help other people do their best.

Another of the several layers making up the text is imagination. Mary constantly challenges her students to respond to questions and issues in imaginative ways. This is important, because if people's imaginations are not engaged, they will fail to see any purpose in what they are doing. Moreover, imagination is hinged to perception. A marvelous quality of this book is how Mary artfully works to help children through imaginative acts to define their place in time. Through the issues they study, the children are encouraged to locate themselves and their time in the course of human history. In the civil rights study that occurs each year, children are helped both to stretch their sense of the present back into the past and to contemplate the future. Through this sense of continuity, realized imaginatively, enduring values are examined. Children learn that the world is something to be questioned and interpreted and, on the other hand, that interpretations of events, today and historically, are multiple and varied. What a person perceives depends in part upon the person doing the viewing. Imaginative effort and intellectual concentration are central to Mary's work, and the connection between imagination, interpretation, and understanding is ever present.

Mary challenges the number one rule of conventional teaching. That is, be busy, up and moving, marching to bells, work, work, work. She advises us to slow down, to reflect on what is happening. In light of the joy and learning that result, when children are engaged in studying content that matters to them, Mary's reasoning convinces. In conventional schooling, children work on acting out someone else's idea, moving like oxen in harness from one page to the next. Consequently, there is little reason for the teacher to attend thoughtfully to the process of how they work. This is a sad aspect of conventional schooling: children choke down a way of doing something engineered by someone else.

Making School by Hand is a celebration of a teacher and her children developing their own way, working by hand. It is a multilayered text rich in meaning. Hopefully, it will play a major role in the ongoing dialogue about the importance of authentic learning.

Ralph Peterson
Arizona State University

Acknowledgments

Before I began writing professionally, I always ignored the acknowledgments in new books I picked up to read. I thought of acknowledgments as something insignificant, irrelevant. In the past few years, as my writing has become more public, I've realized that without the people mentioned in the acknowledgments, a book would never reach fruition.

As I reflect on those I wish to recognize for helping me with *Making School by Hand*, the word *family* comes to mind. My parents, Jimmy and Jan Kenner, gave me the childhood which allowed my hands to begin making things and then stepped aside to allow the creations to come forth. My brothers, Mick and Pat, and my sister Jane shared that childhood. As we've become adults, they have encouraged my work through their love and continued playful sense of humor. I am especially grateful to my brother Mick for providing the mountain retreat the summer I began this book.

This work was furthered also by my husband, Bill, and my daughters, Sarah and Astraea. They have learned over the years what I need to complete my various projects and have given me the time and space to do so. Bill, especially, has helped me get over feeling guilty for needing to be alone to do my work. He is my sounding board and most helpful critic, and I am ever indebted to him for the wisdom he daily directs my way. Additionally, I am supported by his parents, Roy and Edith Glover, who consistently remind me of the importance of family.

Beyond my immediate family, I have been nurtured and guided by several people in my personal and professional life. My friend and spiritual teacher, Erma Pounds, showed me a way to use my hands and heart to make a school. Through her example, she has directly and indirectly helped me shape my life into one of service to others, and she has reminded me to make full use of the gifts that were my birthright. My other mentor, Ralph Peterson, has demonstrated repeatedly how to push the edges of what is possible in education and in living. Ralph has taught me how to be a teacher and how to be a thinker. He never stops caring and wondering how schools could be better for children, and he has influenced me to live my teaching life similarly.

My work as a writer, in particular, has also reaped many benefits from my correspondence and friendships with Vivian Paley and Georgia Heard. Both Vivian and Georgia have encouraged me to keep using my writer's voice, to speak the truths of my heart. Pat Carini has influenced my thinking as an educator. I have found her ideas about reflection on childhood particularly helpful in this book's evolution. My colleagues and dear friends Linda Sheppard, Maryann Eeds, and Elaine Surbeck have kept me pondering the important issues we face as teachers, and at the same time have enabled me to laugh in moments when humor was hard to find. And Elsie Moore-Smith, my fellow teacher and friend on many levels, has inspired me through the example of her own life to remain tenaciously strong even during the most difficult times. She taught me never to give up trying to make our world a better place for all beings who reside here.

On a daily basis, the staff, children, and parents at Awakening Seed School have been a part of my extended family. Through their antics and stories, questions and surprises, they have taught me to come to school each day with a sense of wonder. Each morning as I'm unloading my car, ready for another day, I can't wait to see what will unfold when I walk through the door. A special thanks to Anne Sager for helping to carry the Seed's vision in its early days, and to Yvonne Mersereau, my co-director, who over the years has kept me on track—and pushed me off the track when it was necessary. Without each and every one at the Seed, there would never have been a handmade school.

Beyond my immediate family and the people in my teaching life, I have been loved and supported by two families, one close by and another far away. I will be indebted forever to my friends Jennifer and Ross Robb and their two wonderful daughters, Shannon and Caitlin (whom you will hear more of in the following pages), for making me a part of their family to the extent they have. In particular, the time I have been able to share with Caitlin will be among the most precious moments of my life. The other family, Annie and Marc Horey and their sons, Jon and Scotty, has shared with me over twenty years of friendship as well as many summer days of inspiration at their home on the coast of Maine. It was in their rustic little "writer's cottage" on Quaker Point that I was able to finally finish this book. Without their friendship and that of the other "Quaker Point cottage people," I would not have been able to make the last effort to dig within myself to find the final words I needed.

Finally, I want to thank my longtime colleague and friend Karen Smith for always celebrating and encouraging my work as a teacher and writer. It was Karen who helped keep this manuscript alive when I was ready to give up on it—along with my career as a writer—by suggesting I send it to NCTE. And to Dawn Boyer, my editor, I extend my gratitude for finding her way back into my writing life through circumstances which were meant to be. Her continual belief in me as a writer and her reminders that what I have to say is important have helped me extend my work far beyond anything I could ever have imagined. To Kurt Austin and Rona Smith, for their help in the book's production phase, I also offer my thanks. For their encouragement, as well as that of everyone in my life, I offer my thanks for the hands that have assisted me with *Making School by Hand*.

Introduction

I t is summer. Three years have passed since I wrote the first words of this book. The summer I started writing it, I left the hot Arizona desert and retreated to my brother's cabin in southern Utah. I took along my computer and a quilt I was making for my friend's baby who was to be born that winter. For a month I spent my mornings drinking tea and looking out over the forest from my upstairs room as I wrote the first chapters. That summer I wrote until I could sit still no longer, and then I would step into my hiking boots and explore the forest trails. I found feathers and wildflowers, and even met a rattlesnake one day. I learned to enjoy being alone. When I returned to the cabin—usually in the late afternoon as the sky was beginning to turn rosy—I sat on the porch steps and stitched the quilt. There was a certain quietness that I will always remember. In that solitude of quiet stitching, I came to know a deeper joy associated with the process of making something by hand. I loved seeing the small sections of quilting accumulate into a larger, more beautiful whole. Each stitch was like a silent blessing for the unborn child I would soon come to know. There would be no other quilt like it—it was a unique expression of everything that was in my heart, created by my very own hands.

Originally I intended to write a book about content studies, how they are inspired and implemented. I thought that other teachers might be able to further their own classroom work by hearing how content studies developed in one teacher's classroom. As my writing progressed, I realized that to talk about content studies it was necessary to describe the context in which they occurred. In order to fully explain how curriculum emerged in my classroom, I would need to provide the history of the school where it came to be. A bit further into the process, I also began thinking about the events in my own life that influenced the making of the school and my teaching practice. To understand the greater issues underlying everything in my school life, I knew I needed to examine and reflect on the roots from which it all grew. I needed to understand how and why the activities which filled my childhood days so significantly influenced the teacher I am today. I knew there had to be a way to connect my past with the present, and ultimately to understand how both would offer possibilities for the future.

For a long time I had difficulty seeing how these ideas fit together. I knew they all needed to be included, but they seemed disjointed and separate. Then one day it all became clear. The metaphor for viewing my teaching life came from the baby quilt I stitched the summer I began the book.

It dawned on me that my work as a teacher has not been so different from that experience of making a quilt. Each day is spent assembling smaller parts—ideas, concepts, subject matter, children's interests, current events—into a greater whole. Each day is a new creation, quite different from the one which came before. Unlike assembly-line manufacturing, however, it is much more than just putting small pieces together. When something is handmade, there are additional elements present—such as love, thoughtfulness, caring, and artistic skill—which elevate the experience into something greater. There is love for the process, for the work, and for the one who will receive the creation when it is finished. There is care in the making and concern for growth of the one who inspired the work (Mayeroff 1971). And within the inspiration lies a natural inclination for the artist to extend his or her craft beyond previous levels of accomplishment because the effort is driven by love.

I believe that teaching can and should be approached with this kind of vision. In order for this to happen, several factors need consideration. First of all, it is evident that if we are to work successfully with children, we need to reflect on the ways in which *we* spent our childhood days—in particular, the small and seemingly insignificant activities we engaged in alone or when grown-ups were nowhere to be found. Reflecting on such activities has not only helped me make connections between two very different times in my life, but has also allowed me to make decisions as a classroom teacher about how my students' time should be used for optimum learning and growth. I find myself more frequently asking whether children would select a certain activity if given a choice. If the answer is no, I try to adjust the plan so that it would be something they'd choose.

Second, I think we need to give consideration to this idea of making things by hand. If we continue to teach as if we are assembly-line workers, we will not further our students—nor will we further ourselves. Over the course of my life, it is apparent that making things with my hands has been a priority. From the early days of building sand castles on the beach or sewing tiny clothes for dolls, my hands have been active in helping to shape the world in which I have grown. As a child, however, it was more than a matter of working with my hands. The process was much more complex, for it involved putting things together—often with other children in the neighborhood—to create worlds to which only we children had access. Using artifacts we made with our hands, as well as language and actions, we created rich imaginary worlds that kept us meaningfully engaged for long periods of time. Out of this experience came an understanding of revision and improvisation. I learned that following dreams and wild ideas could lead not only to fun, but also to wonderful surprises. Surprises led to other surprises, opening up possibilities well beyond my original thinking. Applying this perspective to teaching could elevate our practice well beyond *our* wildest dreams and expectations.

A third consideration is how we organize our learning in relation to others. Sometimes learning is better when we have others to share it with us. I see evidence of this every day at school, as members of my classroom work hard to help each other learn new things and celebrate accomplishments and discoveries. On the other hand, I have discovered that time alone is also essential for developing qualities that contribute to creativity, intuition, thoughtfulness, and inspiration. For in the quietness of times when we have just ourselves to contend with, we have an opportunity to touch the deeper aspects of who we are. As a child I had ample time to spend with other children, but I also managed to make time to be alone. When I was young, I spent a good portion of my solitary time creating sanctuaries for myself, both outdoors and within the privacy of my own room. Each of the sanctuaries was a project, made by hand, incorporating ideas that came along to serve a purpose I had in mind. Most projects led to other projects, inspired by a need or idea I wanted to see materialized in some tangible form—which leads to a fourth consideration.

If we are to begin viewing school as a handmade process, we have to give our students daily opportunities to use their hands to help them construct an understanding of what they come upon in the world. We need to trust that, in giving them time to express what they know and to explore ideas they wonder about, they will lead us to new ways of thinking about our work as teachers. In doing so, together we can make a project of our school life.

If we want to take seriously this notion of making a project of our school life, there is one additional idea to ponder which I learned the summer I gave myself the gift of an author's retreat. As teachers we need balance in our lives. We need to devote ourselves to our teaching practice, but we also need to walk away from it at times. During the month I spent writing in Utah, I not only found time to write and think about teaching, but I also allowed time for the adventurer and the artist in myself to come alive. In my weeks of solitude, as the book developed, I saw how necessary each part of myself was for balance and for the furthering of the other parts. This has become evident to me both as a person and as a classroom teacher. If we want to have more to give to our students, we also need to give time to ourselves. When this happens, the projects in which we involve our lives are infinitely richer and more rewarding. This book is the story of a project that has become my life work. It was made by hand (by many hands) and has grown organically from the hearts and minds of people who love to learn together in personal and private ways. It is a story of how childhood interests can blossom into a lifetime profession. It's about making decisions to include the kinds of activities in classrooms that lead to surprises and discoveries. And finally, it is an example of one classroom in one school where the curriculum is specifically designed by and for its daily participants. In sharing this story, it is my hope and dream that others will find a way to use their own hands to make a project of their classrooms—and invite their students to join them in an important, inspiring process.

A Long Way from the Doughnut Shop

When I was eight, I wanted to work in a bakery when I grew up. I had a friend named Mrs. Wilcox who worked at the local bakery. As often as I could, I'd drop by to visit her after school. I loved the black-and-white checkerboard floor and the bakery's warmth. She was warm, too, and I was enthralled by her soft braid of graying hair piled neatly on top of her head. Even more than that, I loved the smells and sights of fresh doughnuts hot out of the fryer, chocolate glazed or sprinkled with sugar. Standing in that bakery, mesmerized by the display cases of sweet pastries, I didn't see how it could get any better.

I swore I would never be a teacher. I was the fourth generation in my family's lineage of teachers, and I wanted something different. I wanted adventure and creativity. I wanted my life work to be fun. When I became a mother, I also realized that I wanted to work with children. So, when I finally made the decision to be a teacher, after considering several other majors in college, I knew I couldn't settle for what was generally available. It quickly became clear that I would have to forge my own way, that my work as a teacher would have to be a "handmade" process. The brief time I spent in traditional schools showed me that I was not cut out for working with curricula and materials that were mass-produced by people only remotely involved in classrooms. Furthermore, I didn't want my own students to experience the years of boredom and limitations I had lived as a child in school.

Somehow I knew my work would have to be created to meet the needs of the specific children before me, taking into account their interests, their world, and my own passions. Out of this awareness grew a school with a living curriculum that has become the creation of the people who inhabit it. Alongside the school and its curriculum, my teaching practice has grown.

To understand how this process has occurred, it's been necessary for me to reflect on the activities and events of my childhood which contributed to my becoming the teacher I am. Eudora Welty (1983) refers to our childhood learning experiences as a series of moments which make up a sort of "pulse"—a pulse that sets the pace for our entire life. In her "Another Way of Looking" workshops, Pat Carini states, "Our own experiences reflected on widens our view." To know who we are, what we believe, and where we are headed, we sometimes have to widen our view by looking back and feeling the pulse of our childhood. This is especially true for teachers. If we care to ask ourselves the questions that will improve our teaching practice, we need to examine the truths of our own childhood. Reflecting on the activities I engaged in as a child has enabled me to see why I have made certain choices in my work as a teacher. It has helped me understand the direction my life has taken and why I have placed importance on specific endeavors. Several questions have arisen in the process:

- What finally lured me away from my dreams of doughnuts?
- What convinced me that I belonged in a classroom with children?
- What influences from my early life were strong enough to inspire the making of a school?
- Why are my most significant childhood memories of events and activities outside of school?
- What made certain activities intrinsically more appealing than others?

As I began to sort out events and memories that would answer these questions, it was evident that school was not so memorable in comparison to my life outside of school. Early on I figured out that if my life was going to be interesting, I would have to create it outside the walls of the classroom. For example, I can remember sitting in boring rows of small, wooden chairs learning to read with Dick and Jane in first grade. But the truly marvelous part was going home and setting up my own tea party (including cupcakes) in the basement—similar to the tea party Sally and Jane had in my red basal reader. Only then did the world of Sally, Dick, and Jane come alive for me. And although I enjoyed making things like jars covered with gold paint-sprayed macaroni, they were nothing like the projects I worked on at home. Life outside of school was so rich with possibility. There was no limit to the expressive opportunities available. Life inside the confines of a classroom failed miserably in comparison.

I think I eventually turned to teaching because I wanted other children to experience the sense of joy and wonder I knew as a child outside of school. But I wanted it to happen *in* school. I wanted them to know what it feels like to create surprising works of art with paints, natural materials, or words. I wanted them to know the excitement of starting a project that no one else suggested and having the time to change and adapt it when a new idea came along. As much as anything, I wanted children to experience school in a different way than I knew it.

It is my belief that children shouldn't have to wait until they're outside of school to be engaged in what interests them. They should be able to involve themselves every day in what matters to them. In *Interest and Effort in Education*, John Dewey wrote, "The problem of educators, teachers, parents, the state, is to provide the environment that induces educative or developing activities, and where these are found the one thing needful in education is secured" (1913). My inspiration to teach and think this way came from something larger than school that I began to learn as a very young child. Although I didn't realize until much later what that something was, I know that everything I've come to value and believe—both in and outside of my teaching life—is rooted in the play that occupied much of my childhood. Reflecting on the play that filled my free time has revealed several significant patterns that have influenced how I teach and live:

◆   I constantly used my hands to make things.
◆   I always had an abundance of raw materials available for both indoor and outdoor play (e.g., wood, sand, mud, fabric, clay, paint, grass).
◆   The things I made were often small and detailed.
◆   Much of my time was spent building sanctuaries.
◆   There was a balance of time alone and time with others.
◆   Much of the play was sustained over long periods of time.
◆   I always dreamed of doing something important with my life, something that would make a difference.

The environment in which I grew up was a significant contributing factor in support of such activities. Both the outdoor surroundings of my childhood and the interior spaces I knew enabled me to develop aspects of myself that would one day set the stage for my work as a school maker and a teacher. Those spaces were sacred to me and I have realized that one of my primary responsibilities as a teacher is to enable children to protect their wonderfully private worlds of childhood by giving them a chance to create their own sacred spaces as well. To insure that this will happen in their everyday lives, I have tried to give them opportunities to create worlds and artifacts similar to those I was able to make as a child. I have tried to give them time to use their hands to make spaces which fill them with that same sense of security I felt when I was young—where they can create, feel safe, and quietly wonder.

When the idea of creating a school first arose, I wanted to be sure that the school would be a place to which children would want to return each fall, not a place they would dread.

It was my intention to establish a setting where children would be inspired and excited about learning, rather than feeling bored and frustrated as I did as a young student. I wanted it to be a place that would suggest wonderful ideas to children (Duckworth 1987), a place where they could express who they are in a variety of ways. Knowing how important it was for me to have the freedom to use my imagination and creativity as a child, I realized that I have a responsibility to help children do the same.

I believe that each child, each human being, has to do this according to his or her own needs. As school makers all we can do is set the stage and provide an environment that supports children and teachers in this process. When the setting is safe and stimulating, children will take ownership of their learning. They will move beyond our expectations of them and show us the way into worlds we have not yet imagined. They will become our teachers and show us the kind of schools and teaching practices necessary for moving ourselves ahead to meet the requirements of our future.

Sanctuary Builder

A Hopi legend says their people first came to this Earth by emerging from a hole in the bottom of the Grand Canyon. They crawled up out of the hole and, after thousands of years of migrations, settled on the high desert mesas just east of the Canyon. Their history is firmly rooted in the northern Arizona land which they still inhabit to this day. When I think of my own life and its history, I sometimes wonder if I too might not have emerged from some hole in the ground. Not in the Grand Canyon of Arizona, but in the field behind my childhood home on the plains of rural Nebraska. My memories, and the roots of the person I have become, are deeply embedded in the grassy land adjacent to my parents' house. The field was an invitation for the children of our neighborhood to join in the celebration of living. It was a four-season playground for our imaginations, a launching pad for adventure. It was our sanctuary.

Within the field we found and created other sanctuaries. Some were made collectively with neighborhood children. Some I made alone. In the winter months, when the temperature was right and the snow had that perfect consistency, we'd spend hours hollowing out the insides of the drifts, making our own version of an igloo. In the warmer months, we found other places to inhabit that were always an integral part of our play. There was a thicket of thorny bushes hollowed out just enough underneath so we could crawl along on our bellies. We hauled in sand from our backyard so the thicket would have a soft, cool floor for us to lie on in the summers. That secluded space became our escape route and primary hiding space during the various games of army, cowboys and Indians, spy, and other variations we *imagined. Although the thorny branches added a treacherous element, that thicket will remain in my memory as one of the havens of our play. It was a space provided by nature where we could hide and take a moment to calm our racing heartbeats. It was a place where we could reflect and think of the next move in our imaginary adventures. Another spot, which I called the wood, was near the thicket, and it was a place for quiet reflection. The wood was a small area of trees with soft, green grass sprouting up from the earth. It was just thick enough to provide shade in the hot summer months and sparse enough to let a cool breeze pass through. It was a place where quiet and magic stirred, where dreams could be dreamed without interruption.*

In and around the field we built a series of houses. One, made collaboratively with the neighbors, was an underground fort which consisted of a huge hole in the ground with long planks across it for a roof and weeds stuck on the top for camouflaging. Five or six children could fit inside it. Other houses appeared from time to time, more ephemeral than the underground fort. One of my favorites was the log house. It was essentially a pile of logs cut for firewood and neatly arranged in a U-shaped configuration. I don't remember it having a roof, but I do recall the smell of the fresh-cut grass we used to carpet the floor. The smell made me want to lie there and soak up its earthiness. When I sat in the log house, I imagined what it would be like to be a pioneer long ago on the dusty Midwestern plains. I thought of the courage it must have taken for the early settlers to face the howling wind that would blow through the cracks in the walls of their homes— hopefully more airtight than my log hut.

There was an assortment of tree houses all over the neighborhood that we migrated to on various occasions. Some were built by our parents, and some we built ourselves. I always liked the ones we built ourselves the best. My personal tree house, constructed mostly of discarded wood my father gave me from time to time, was an ongoing project—always under continual revision. It was a good space for just one or two people.

One other structure, which I built myself, became the perfect place for my private thoughts. It was a small red-brick house, not more than five feet square, with walls about three feet high. I meticulously laid the bricks in an alternating pattern without the benefit of mortar. The house had a doorway and two windows with a board across the top of each window, forming a primitive lintel. I must have *used long boards across the top for the roof. The brick house was dark and cool inside. It had a sandy floor covered with an old tapestry rug. There was a flap over the doorway. I spent many hours sitting or lying by myself in the brick house. It felt like a cocoon. What stays in my mind about the brick house after all these years is how secure and secluded I felt when I was inside it. The cool dampness was soothing, and I cherished any moment I could be there. Looking back, I can see that it was perhaps the first space I consciously created for myself that was specifically available for reflection. In the brick house, I first experienced the blessing of silence and the security of knowing that in moments of absolute quiet there could be inner peace and inspiration.*

Years later I have come to see that building the brick house was practice for the work I would eventually choose. In a sense, the brick house has become a metaphor for the school I have made with the help of others. Through the process of creating my brick sanctuary as a child, my hands and heart and mind showed me the importance of private, safe spaces for all children.

Like making my childhood sanctuaries, making a school has been a long-term process. I have discovered that a school doesn't grow overnight. It takes a long time to become the kind of place that inspires and nurtures children. A school where children *want* to be every day, because it is a safe and interesting environment, requires many years of careful tending before it reaches maturity. It takes considerable reflection on childhood events by those responsible for its growth to become an established sanctuary for learners. For a school to serve as a place of possibility, there must be remembering and, at the same time, a vision for the future. When our school began, we made sure that our vision was well supported by what we had learned from our experiences as children in school.

Awakening Seed began as an idea offered by my wise friend Erma Pounds, who had a vision of a school where children of all walks of life could come together to study and learn from each other—where differences would be celebrated and a sense of harmony and understanding could serve as a model for world peace. Before my own children were born,

I used to listen to her speak of this school and think that someday I'd like them to attend such a school. Over the course of several years, my interest in the school remained. Finally, after many inquiries on my part, Erma suggested that I start the school. So, in 1977 Awakening Seed began with nine children under the age of five, in the garage of my home. My friend Anne Sager and I combined the assortment of children we were each babysitting (including my own three-year-old and six-month-old daughters) and began three mornings a week to make a school by hand.

The first few years were a continual process of vision and revision. Although we were just beginning, several thoughts were clear to us and became the seeds of our philosophical principles. They evolved from both our experiences as children in school, and from observations of our own young students:

◆ Children learn best when they are given a chance to use all of their senses to educate their minds (Dewey 1915).

◆ Everyday life and real-life activities must be included in the school curriculum in order for it to be meaningful and interesting to children.

◆ The needs and interests of both children and teachers should occupy a central position in the development and implementation of curriculum.

◆ The stories of children provide a rich insight into their lives as well as a vehicle for self-expression, imagination, humor, and sharing of common thoughts or feelings.

◆ The arts must be included in the daily lives of school-children as a way for them to let the world know who they are and what they aspire to be, and to keep their creative spirit alive (Mearns 1929).

◆ A school's vision must be all-encompassing and include ways to help children develop an awareness of their integral role as citizens of our planet.

◆ Children need opportunities to learn to value the preciousness of life and all life-forms.

◆ Development of a sense of community within classrooms and schools should be a foremost concern of teachers and school makers.

◆ By honoring and celebrating our differences as well as our similarities, we can enrich all of our lives and overcome hurtful prejudices (Derman-Sparks 1989).

We had no money, only my daughters' toys, and a great deal of enthusiasm with which to create a school. In those days it was our vision of possibilities that kept us inspired. Our wise teacher and friend continually offered us thoughts such as these to sustain our work:

Some Thoughts on Working with Children

That there is a growing need for work among children has been demonstrated, especially of late. Children are being born who will require us to give them the foundations upon which they can build structures of vaster proportions than we have dreamed of. Theirs will be a higher knowledge, and they will have to fulfill the work that we have begun.

Each will have a different work because of varying natures; so the method should conform to the nature of the child.

Meet a child half-way, and both child and teacher are taught.

Reverse the usual order of the child-life, and instead of heaping treasures upon it, let it first learn that it must give, and that what it gives is considered of value. With this incentive held out, the real child-life develops, and its whole nature opens to receive instruction.

Material gifts then have a broader significance, and the idea of "I must have" is done away with, and in its place is substituted the controlling thought of the higher life, "I must serve."

Our best workers should be teachers of children, for the child is nearest to the sage, the sage is nearest to the child, and it takes a sage to understand true simplicity.

A child wants to be taken for what it is, not for what we are.

Let the children be taught that they are co-workers with each other and with us, and that their work is needed, and half the problem is solved. The rest will follow of itself, and an army of children will be formed that will become the warriors of the future for saving of humanity.

—author unknown

We wanted something different, a school where human values and respect for our planet were at the core of the curriculum. We wanted art and music and gardening and happiness to be an integral part of our days together, as well as reading and writing and math. Our intention was to create a sanctuary where we could all feel safe to explore and wonder about life. A primary goal of ours was to help our young students appreciate the world around them, including each other, all living creatures, and the planet itself.

One way in which we did this was through studies of the environment. For example, in 1981 a group of four- to seven-year-olds visited a water treatment plant to see where water from our homes went. After reading Bill Pete's *The Wump World*, the story of creatures whose world is nearly destroyed by outer-space invaders called Pollutions, the students produced a short film of the story out on the school lawn. That same year they wrote letters to their congressional representatives asking them to support the Clean Air Act. My daughter Sarah, age seven, wrote to Senator Barry Goldwater, "I want you to tell your Senator friends to vote for the Clean Air Act. I won't breathe the air, because it is polluted." Her friend Beth, also seven, began her letter to Secretary of the Interior James Watt, "Dear Secretary James Watt, You better get your act together." Others pleaded with the Japanese Embassy to stop killing whales.

In 1985, when starvation in Africa became a topic of discussion, five-year-old Jaymie wrote a short but poignant piece in response (see Figure 1). That same spring our school raised nearly $1,000 with a garage sale one day to help feed starving children in Ethiopia. Among the recycled items for sale were handmade books such as Jaymie's that the children had made for the occasion.

Whenever we could, we attempted to help the children see not only how their lives connected to the world, but how they could make a difference. As our school grew bigger, we learned that even though we were very small in relation to the rest of the planet, we each have an important part to play. We came to see that we are collectively and individually valuable members of the human race.

Figure 1   A page from Jaymie's book *Hunger*. Her text reads: "Some kids are dying for food."

We learned quite early in our school's evolution to make time for what children brought to school from their everyday lives. We realized that we'd be missing out on important learning if we ignored these daily offerings from our students. By paying attention to their interests and needs, we were able to create a curriculum which was not only interesting but also relevant to their lives. In addition to bringing children's lives into school, we ventured out into the world to see what we could see. During the school's first year, when one child's father took a job as manager of a large Phoenix hotel, we loaded up our nine preschoolers, hopped on the city bus, and headed downtown to check it out. We rode up the escalator, visited the revolving restaurant, and looked out over the city

from the hotel's glass elevator. Another time we visited a city
landfill and a local electrical power plant. When I was first
introduced to the idea of making handmade books, we took a
field trip to a public school library where the handmade
books of child authors were on display. This visit inspired our
very young authors to make their own books.

During one study of whales and dolphins, we didn't let
our residency in the desert limit our learning possibilities. In
fact, we learned that jojoba oil, derived from a desert plant,
actually was being used as a substitute for whale oil in products such as cosmetics. Although we couldn't see marine
wildlife firsthand, we were able to visit a factory where jojoba
beans were being processed into oil. Just as we encouraged
the children to bring their life interests to school, we tried to
show them ways in which the world around them could
become a part of their everyday lives. By designing the curriculum this way, we were able to model the kind of lifelong
learners we wanted them to be.

Our practice of encouraging children to experience the
world involved giving them opportunities to learn by using all
of their senses. I have few memories from my early school
years, and I believe this is true, in part, because my classmates and I seldom used all our senses for learning. We saw
and heard things, but rarely did we further our understanding
through taste, touch, or smell. When Anne and I started our
school, we made it a priority to give our students as many
opportunities as possible to know the world through their
senses. They played with sand, baked cookies, and listened
to the sounds of desert birds. One day, because Arizona children have so little experience with ice and snow, we bought
a large block of ice. The children squealed with delight as
they each took a turn standing barefoot on it. When the ice
had melted, we painted, drew, and wrote stories about our
giant ice cube. The stories were another way we learned to
share who we were with each other.

One thing we learned quickly was to pay attention to
children's stories. Our early days of listening to stories and
recording them for our young students laid a foundation for

the language arts curriculum that has emerged at our school. When a child came in with a story to tell, we quickly wrote it down and often encouraged him or her to illustrate it. At the end of each year, every child had a collection of recorded stories to read over and over. As we listened to their stories, we realized ways to develop the direction of studies, further expressive opportunities, and facilitate reading and writing. Their stories not only revealed ways to develop our teaching and to know the children's interests and thoughts, but also provided us with a source of humor—a necessary element in the early stages of establishing a school. Probably the most legendary funny story (and my favorite) originated from four-year-old Joshua in 1980. One day his mother approached me and asked, "If I supply the paper, would you write out and make a copy of what you do each day? I'm having trouble getting a straight story out of Joshua." I was curious about what he was telling his mother. She continued, "Yesterday he reported this: 'There was a wild herd of cabbages coming out of the quiet corner! We had to eat the cabbages all morning and walk on them all morning! Then they blasted into Mary's room and Mary asked what these cabbages were doing in her room. All the children glared and some blasted into my room. We had to eat them all morning for snack and lunch.'"

Joshua's story—now a permanent volume in our school library, along with hundreds of others from our students—not only kept us laughing, but was a reminder of the surprises and richness that come to our lives when we listen to what children say. Listening to the children's stories was a way for us to celebrate life, to see its joys and its wild possibilities. This was quite a contrast from my own school experience. The stories I wanted to tell never seemed to be appreciated. My most vivid memory from kindergarten serves as an example of the difference.

On the last day of March, my sister was born. We had a tradition in the kindergarten that when it was a special day, such as your birthday or if your sister had just been born, you got to wear "the crown." It was a way to honor big days in our lives. We also had another tradition: if you were naughty or if you misbehaved (i.e., if you talked too much), you had to sit in one of those little wooden chairs behind the piano. On the day my sister was born, I did some time behind the piano—wearing the crown. The problem I seemed to have in school was that the scenarios in my mind were infinitely more interesting than what was going on in the classroom. I had stories to tell, but there was no acceptable outlet for them. Besides, what was happening at school was, for the most part, boring. When I was bored, I talked, and my teachers didn't always appreciate my well-developed verbal skills. As we developed our school, we made every effort to include opportunities throughout the day for children to share their stories through talk, writing, and art.

The few pleasant memories I have of elementary school all involve the arts. Whether it was the music teacher who pushed aside the desks and chairs to teach us the Virginia reel, or the rare projects we were allowed to create with our own hands, it was the opportunity to use our expressive nature that mattered. When Anne and I started Awakening Seed, we wanted to be sure to include more of these memorable experiences. For that reason, the arts have remained a significant part of our school, and they have frequently been attached to the stories children have brought with them from home each day. In fact, the arts have received as much attention as reading, writing, and mathematics. For some children, the arts have provided their most meaningful way to belong.

In 1979, we moved out of my garage and into a rented facility, but even as the school grew, we worked hard to maintain the family atmosphere of our first two years. Without knowing it consciously, we had established ourselves as a small learning community, and we didn't want to lose that feeling. As more students joined us in the years after that, we tried to remain true to our original vision. We made sure everyone felt safe and comfortable in our school setting.

This view of schooling was a far cry from my second-grade experience in which my teacher was an old-school disciplinarian who abhorred talkers. When I talked out of turn in her class, I was invited to stand at the chalkboard with my nose in a chalk-drawn circle—located just high enough on the board that I had to stand on my tiptoes. Her disciplinary tactics did little to support a sense of community in our class and, in fact, were even less effective in controlling the talking problem. Children were not encouraged to develop their voices or establish themselves as a community (Glover and Sheppard 1989). Rather, they were required to be silent. In the process of making *our* school, we wanted children's voices to be heard. As a result of our efforts, a community was born. Members of the school community felt confident about taking risks and sharing themselves with others. As each child or teacher became a stronger individual, the group as a whole was strengthened. My personal history as a student included very little of this type of thinking on the part of teachers or administrators. The notion of forcing children to conform was a theme running through much of my early school life. An experience from seventh grade provides a significant example.

I had a teacher who, in retrospect, was well meaning and good hearted, but for some reason he decided it was his mission in life to transform us from the hormonal savages we were into fine upstanding citizens. He undertook this process through the 7Cs Club. The seven Cs—character, courtesy, cooperation, citizenship, carefulness, conduct, and cheerfulness—were offered as beacons for finding our way out of the darkness of our uncivilized lives. We elected officers and held monthly meetings which required flower arrangements, a candelabra (seven candles for the seven Cs), and our finest dress clothes. I'm not sure what the purpose of these meetings was, except perhaps to practice orderly conduct as members of the human race. A feature of the monthly meetings was the selection of one girl and one boy as model citizens for that month. When a student was picked (by the teacher, of course), he or she was awarded a badge. The badge, to be worn at all subsequent meetings, consisted of a blue ribbon with a gold seal on it. I sweated it out until February before I was chosen. At the end of the year we had our big extravaganza, the crowning of the king and queen of the 7Cs Club.

I was not selected as the queen of the 7Cs Club. Perhaps my reputation as another C, chatterbox, prevented me from attaining the highest honor. At least I received a monthly badge. Years later, I wonder how the kids who were never picked for anything felt. I wonder if their failure to make it in the 7Cs Club has affected their lives as real citizens. How did it influence their sense of belonging to a community?

Interestingly enough, when I recently tried to recall all of the 7Cs, I was certain that one of them was cleverness. I was surprised to discover that this quality was not included among the sacred seven. Then I remembered that this same teacher who had concocted his own plan for shaping citizens of the future had once told me I was clever. *Clever* stayed in my mind. I think about this, especially when I am faced with a student who challenges the classroom's status quo. When I see a young artist who can't sit still through reading, stares off into space at math time, and then spends hours adding details to a diorama of his desert mammal, I remember *clever*. If I learned anything from my eccentric seventh-grade teacher, it's that many times what you think you're teaching isn't really what you're teaching at all. He thought he was molding me into a fine citizen by giving me a blue and gold badge for good behavior. The badge I continue to carry with me as an adult is cleverness. Certainly being a good citizen is important to me, but it is cleverness that has provided the most interesting surprises for me—as a teacher, as an artist, and as a writer. I realized then that good citizens keep the world running smoothly, but clever folks make life significantly more interesting. When we started our school, we wanted to make sure that cleverness had its honored place among the many qualities we were fostering in our students.

This experience helped me realize that embedded in the curriculum must be a way for individuals to be celebrated within the school community. Over the years we have tried to do just that. We have honored the differences and unique qualities in children and teachers. Jewish families have been invited to share the stories and traditional foods of Passover, Rosh Hashanah, and Hanukkah. Native American parents have come to show us artifacts and ceremonies of their people. African American children have stood alongside their parents as they talked of their experiences growing up prior to the Civil Rights Movement. A boy in a wheelchair was featured with his classmates in a dance production of Chris Van Allsburg's book *Jumanji*. Children who have challenges as readers have learned to enjoy the world of books alongside their peers, who often serve as tutors.

Throughout Awakening Seed's existence, celebration of the individual within a community of supportive friends has been a priority. From our school's very first days, we have always considered the diversity within our school population to be one of its strengths. By honoring each person's unique qualities we have come to understand in a deeper way how we are all connected. As our school has grown from a small group of preschoolers in my family garage to an established learning community, we have come to appreciate what we have created together. From the days of having to pack up everything we owned on the weekends and storing it inside locked cupboards because we shared the facility with others, we have learned to appreciate the space we now call our own. Since 1986 we have been settled in a location where we can leave our art on the walls and not have to worry about moving furniture around to accommodate others, so we have been able to focus on developing the program in new ways. We've been able to do more ongoing projects, develop our libraries, and display our learning on the walls for more than five days. Our school has begun to feel like home. One visiting parent, considering Awakening Seed for her son, said the school resembled a much lived-in family room—one where people were happily busy with the tasks of daily living. She ended up choosing our school, not because we had slick storage cabinets and tidy, antiseptic classrooms, but because it was a place where people lived. To me that was one of the highest compliments paid to our school. Like the sanctuaries I built for myself as a child, it has become a haven for dreams and visions to come alive. For in creating an environment where people feel comfortable, safe, and happy, we find that the opportunities for learning hold infinite possibilities.

CHAPTER THREE

Composing Community

Behind our house, in a section of land that separated our yard from
the field, there was a row of poplar trees. It ran the entire length of
our backyard, perhaps 150 feet. There was a watering ditch along the
row of trees. For as many years as I can remember, until I was sent
off to summer camp, a phenomenon would occur with that ditch and
the children in our neighborhood. Each day, after assorted other activities had happened—baseball practice, swimming lessons, or trips to
the library—a question would fly around the neighborhood: What
time is "the stream" going to run? Once a time was established, the
reply traveled just as quickly, and soon children appeared for our
favorite daily event. We turned on the garden hose at one end of the
trees in a spot that came to be known as the dam. Essentially, it was
a huge hole that had eroded in the small hillside, thanks to our years
of running the hose there. The dam was our reservoir for the hours of
play ahead. We carefully monitored how much water would run
down the stream. Nestled under the trees—much like the children of
Roxaboxen (McLerran 1991)—we created a community of water,
sand, mud, grass, and rocks. In addition to the natural substances,
we incorporated plastic army men, die-cast metal cars (which my
father, to this day, is still digging up), and scraps of wood for houses
and bridges. Each day, as the water flowed through the heart of our
imaginary village, we created a world where people could come and
go, inventing lives and a living environment. I spent hours arranging
a tiny hillside along the water. I'd take a crayon and draw doors and
windows on a block of wood which would be carefully placed in the
hillside as a split-level house. Small rocks were placed neatly near the

*house to designate a driveway for the various vehicles that would
carry imaginary visitors to my home. Sometimes little plastic boats, or
more rustic ones of wood and paper, would venture down the stream.
Each day became a revision of the previous one.*

The significance of running the stream was multidimensional. On a basic level, it was an enjoyable time for
us to be outside, playing with the available raw materials. The opportunity to continue the play over a long period
of time allowed us to extend and develop the idea of a community. On a deeper level, the stream immersed us in the
experience of being a community. When I think of how my
teaching has evolved, I believe that this single childhood
experience, above all others, has influenced what I do to
build and support community in my classroom. The process
of composing and creating with mud and sand gave me a
way to think about how to use time to help learners feel like
they belonged and had ideas that mattered to others. It taught
me that when time is given for ideas and people to grow
together, wonderful and exciting things happen.

The stream also gave us a chance to experience firsthand
the idea of revision. In running it every day, we were able to create something of our own that had meaning for us, that we could
control. As we talked to negotiate the daily revisions to our village of sand and water, a strong, unspoken sense of camaraderie
grew among us. We learned to listen to each other's ideas and
apply them if they would enhance our current work. We saw
how small changes could directly affect our community work in
positive ways. We also learned to settle differences when suggested revisions might damage the whole. Through a common
project, we sustained our commitment to working together for a
long period of time. It was as if we functioned as one mind.
What we became and what we created as a group was much
greater than what we could have done as individuals. Those
summer days held a richness that remains to this day. It was, as
Alice McLerran (1991) describes her mother's childhood experience, "a celebration of the active imagination, of the ability of

children to create, even with the most unpromising materials, a world of fantasy so real and multidimensional that it earns a lasting place in memory." It was an experience not only filled with memories, but one which has filtered up through my life in the classroom and touched each and every day.

The lessons I learned from the stream about revision were among the most valuable for my work, particularly during the first ten years of our school's existence when we had to do so much moving around. During those years I learned a whole lot more than how to be a teacher. Among other things, I became a fairly accomplished painter and drywaller (it must have been all that experience with mud in the stream). We all became practiced movers, continually revising the space we inhabited.

Once the physical needs of our school had been met for the most part, we were able to devote more of our attention to curriculum development. Although we always provided our students with wonderful learning experiences, our new space gave us the chance to grow in ways that had been impossible previously. Each year I have taught, I've tried to choose one area of the curriculum upon which to focus my thoughts. As the years have accumulated, different aspects of our classroom life have received the necessary attention. Among them has been the development of content studies.

I have come a long way in how I've learned to use content in my classroom. At Awakening Seed we have deliberately avoided using textbooks and have developed studies according to what we have valued as important. In my earlier teaching years, I would often plan out the entire year in short, one- or two-week units of study. I allowed a little time for lots of topics—all chosen by me. Some years I would take a broad concept, such as cycles or neighbors, and tie the entire year together in that way. The problem with such a process was that it didn't give us the flexibility to explore material at a deeper level because we were always moving on to something else. There was always a sense of needing to hurry ourselves along because something else was waiting to be covered.

At some point, my thinking shifted. I started thinking of ways to give studies more time to develop, to go deeper into what was before us. I also began to pay more attention to what my students were interested in and to listen to what and how they wanted to learn. Through this process I have made several observations about content studies:

◆   They have evolved in different ways. Some studies are included each school year because we believe the content is significant. For example, each January and February my class is involved in a study of civil rights. It generally begins with the life of Martin Luther King Jr. and can take any direction from there. One year we ended up studying Africa. Another year we became fascinated with the Underground Railroad and the life of Harriet Tubman. Regardless of the specific focus, it always ties back to issues related to civil rights.

◆   Sometimes studies arise from personal interests, either of mine or of the children. The summer I spent a month in Utah, I became more aware of birds and was fascinated with their habits, their feathers, and their nests. I thought a study of birds would be an interesting way to begin the year. When I presented the idea to the children, they wanted a broader study. So we settled with a three-month study of creatures that fly, which included flying dinosaurs, bees and wasps, the mythical winged horse Pegasus, birds, and butterflies. In this way, the study began from a personal interest but was expanded and developed to meet individual needs of children. They were given a voice in how the content study was conducted.

◆   Other studies have developed in response to local and world issues. When recycling and environmental awareness began receiving a resurgence of attention, it made sense for us to pursue these topics at a school level. The focus began with what we could do personally to help the environment, such as recycling and picking up trash. It grew into a study of natural resources, endangered species, and conservation. It was a matter of reaching out to the world and bringing life into the classroom for further examination.

◆   Many studies grow from the people who make up each
    classroom. It has always been important at our school to
    include children and families with varied ethnic and
    socioeconomic backgrounds. We develop curriculum and
    content studies to incorporate the rich traditions children
    bring to our school. For example, one year a K–1 class had
    children with families of Native American, African, Indian,
    Colombian, Japanese, Mexican, Israeli, and Slavonian her-
    itage. Not wanting to miss out on the wealth of possibili-
    ties, the teacher devoted an entire semester to studying
    each culture. They tasted food, made artifacts, read books,
    and learned songs from each wonderful tradition. Their
    family roots became the curriculum.

◆   There are other times when content studies arise unexpect-
    edly. Events in the world, in children's and teachers' lives,
    demand attention. When Magic Johnson announced his
    retirement from professional basketball because he had
    contracted the HIV virus, the news could not be ignored.
    The children raised questions that needed answers, which
    led to other questions that wouldn't go away. In time, the
    questions evolved into a study of the entire human body.

Regardless of how specific content becomes part of the
curriculum, it is a process somewhat like constructing a bridge
to be used for entering new and unexplored territory. We use
our hands, our hearts, and minds to build the structures which
allow us to embark on adventures with others in a way we seldom travel alone. The content studies in my classroom are
those adventures. The adventure is in traveling to the unknown;
and it is also in the planning and preparation for the journey, as
well as the building process itself. We construct our curriculum
from the children's ideas and the connections they make
between their thoughts and experiences. Experiences come
from books we read, places we visit (real or imagined), and discussions that follow. For example, when we studied the human
body and learned that muscles atrophy when they aren't used,
Robert asked, "Is that what happened to Colin in *The Secret
Garden?*" The conversations that arise from experiences we

share as a class allow the children to reach new understanding. The talk and exchanging of ideas give them further building materials from which to construct learning.

One of the most exciting aspects of making our own curriculum is seeing how children put things together and continue to tie them back to previous experiences, much as my neighborhood comrades and I spent summers doing just that with our stream. A conversation that occurred in my classroom one day demonstrates this point well. During a discussion of Harriet Tubman's life, we learned that as a runaway slave she followed the Big Dipper and the North Star to find her way north to freedom. Some of my first and second graders were unfamiliar with these stars, so their homework assignment was to locate them in the night sky. I began the next day by asking, "Did anyone find the Big Dipper and the North Star last night?"

Drew was anxious to report his findings. He had brought in his glow-in-the-dark book of constellations to show the class what the Big Dipper and North Star look like. Leor brought a plastic beach ball with constellations on it as a resource for the discussion. Russell's visual aid was a star map of the January evening skies. After we identified the configuration and explained the relationship between the Big Dipper and the North Star, Rose said, "The North Star is called Polaris. I just read it in *On the Day You Were Born.*" Russell, engrossed in his star map, appeared disinterested in the discussion. When he heard Rose's comment, he looked up from his map and said, "I just noticed that Polaris is the tip of the handle of the Little Dipper!" Then Abraham, who had been studying the drawing of the Big Dipper and North Star on the chalkboard, declared, "It's a flag." I asked him to explain, and again he said, "It's a flag."

I asked a child to bring me the "F" encyclopedia, and sure enough, it was the flag of Alaska. "How did you know that, Abe?"

"We learned it in summer school last year."

Discovering that the Big Dipper and North Star were indeed on the flag of Alaska, I requested the "A" encyclopedia for further information. We found out that the flag was designed by a thirteen-year-old boy. The seven stars of the dipper represent gold mining in Alaska, and the eighth star, the North Star, is included because Alaska is located so far north. When I read this information, I noticed a few blank faces in the crowd, so we pulled out the globe and located Alaska and the Arctic Circle on it.

Meanwhile someone asked, "What's that star close to the moon at night?" When I replied that it is the planet Venus, Danielle said, "We learned in our research last year that when Venus was first discovered, people thought it was a bright star." When she said this, Russell rejoined the conversation, offering, "I see here on the map that the closest constellation to Venus is the Great Square of Pegasus." At the mention of Pegasus, Rose and Danielle lit up. The mythical winged horse Pegasus had been one of their most recent passions. And there it was, appearing again in a discussion that started with a runaway slave.

Discussions such as this one are not unusual in classrooms where content and conversation are plentiful. When our days are filled with opportunities to actively construct answers to questions which arise, everyone is inspired to learn more. If we empower children to work and think this way in school, to approach learning much the same way an artist approaches his or her craft, we are giving them an experience that has lifelong implications. By learning to compose their school lives, they are given an opportunity to practice composing their lives in general. And if they know that their ideas, dreams, and curiosities are honored and encouraged, they are likely to do as the ancient poet was said to do: mount his winged horse Pegasus, inspired to write, to create, and to wonder.

This kind of learning rises up from the foundation built by people who share scholarly pursuits. The layers of study and conversation, which are an integral part of a classroom that operates this way, take many weeks and months to cultivate. The connections emerge from class studies, stories read, projects worked on, and conversations about daily living. They begin on the very first day of school.

A Blueprint for Living and Learning

When I was four, my brother Mick and I, along with our four-year-old neighbor, were invited to attend the nursery school held by the home-ec students at the high school. It was my first school experience. We'd recently had carpet installed in our living room at home, and my mother gave us the scraps to play with. We had invented some sort of army game that required large belts which we made out of the thick rubber carpet padding. We insisted on wearing these to our first day of school. We wanted to bring our adventure along with us. The only adventure I can remember at the nursery school, however, happened to one of the other preschool girls. While sitting in one of those little old-fashioned wooden chairs with the round spokes on the back, she managed to get her arm stuck between the spokes. No matter what the teachers tried, they couldn't get her arm unstuck from the chair. Finally they brought in the maintenance man with a saw, who cut the spokes to free her arm. It was real-life drama with a real person using real tools for a real purpose.

My first day of school was memorable, not because of anything that the teachers taught me, but because something significant happened that grabbed my attention. I've always wanted my students to walk away from their first day of school feeling the same way, except I have wanted their memories to be impressed with what we've begun to create as a community. Like my preschool cronies and I who brought our carpet belts along on the first day, I've realized that each student arrives at school with his or her

own adventures in hand. My job as their teacher is to incorporate what they bring with them into our everyday classroom living. Additionally, I know it is my responsibility to
clear the way for other adventures we will have together.

Beginning school each year is not unlike preparing for a
trek into the wilderness. Supplies must be gathered, and everything has to be in place for a safe and fulfilling adventure.
Checklists remind me of everything that has to be done before
we can take our first step. Previous years of teaching serve as
my compass, but they also carry the knowledge that no two
years are ever alike. As a teacher, I feel like I have to be ready
for anything and everything. My head is full of questions:

◆ How will this group be different from last year's class?

◆ How will they be the same?

◆ How shall we begin?

◆ What should we pursue as our first study of the year?

◆ Can I really do this for another year?

◆ How can I balance the time needed for basic academic
work with that required for all the creative projects that
everyone enjoys?

◆ How can I give children more choice in shaping their
education?

◆ What surprises await me this year?

Each September I rehearse over and over in my mind
how the beginning of school will go. I know that spontaneous
events will eventually play a major role in determining the
course of our school year, but I also understand the importance of starting with a plan. Years in the classroom have
shown me that the first weeks of school, essentially, become
the blueprint for how we will conduct ourselves in the coming
months. In fact, the process of establishing this blueprint
becomes our first content work of the year. Although each year
is different and impossible to predict, there are always consis-
tent elements which actually appear on the first day of school.

First, the children and I gather on the floor by the chalkboard. There is an abundance of energy in the room, which

feels somewhat like a volcano about to erupt. Children join
the circle with new shoes that still have treads on the soles.
Eyebrows are visible, thanks to end-of-summer haircuts. The
brightness of the children's colorful clothing is outshone only
by the anticipation in their eyes. We settle down to attend to
the first line of business, making up our class rules. All of the
usual items are listed for proper conduct: Be kind. Work hard.
Do your best. Don't run in the room. Be a good listener.
Don't bother other people., etc. This year one child suggests,
"Be appropriate." I ask him to elaborate. He proceeds to
explain his personal efforts during the past school year to use
appropriate behavior. He wants it to be included in this year's
plan. So we add his suggestion to our list.

When the list meets everyone's satisfaction, we move on
to an examination of our immediate environment. I ask the
children to take their clipboards and sketch things of interest.
They disperse like ants, hungry to know their surroundings.
The woodworking area and sewing machine are popular items
for Margaret and Deanna. Stefanie sketches the chart rack that
holds our brand new class rules (see Figure 2). Each child also
draws a small self-portrait to decorate our door. A mural of the
class is constructed as the first of many art projects that will
cover the bare September walls. Slowly the energy subsides as
everyone settles in and we begin our journey together.

Each new year a few general themes surface. Routines
need to be established. Children have to learn where things
are located, how to do the various chores around the classroom, and how to master procedures such as borrowing
books from school. Initially establishing ourselves as a community requires a considerable amount of group conversation. One frequently discussed issue is how we use time.
During these conversations we deal with classroom issues,
but our discussion often spills over into real-life applications
as well. In one early morning discussion about fooling
around, Aaron commented, "Every job you have in the real
world has to do with school." Robert said, "No, it has to do
with getting an education." They were both getting at the
same thing: if you don't learn and put your best self into your

Stefanie's drawing of the class rules from the first day of school.   Figure 2

work, you won't be able to get a good job. In other words, get serious about school work.

One of the biggest challenges of the early part of the school year is not only talking about issues such as how we use time, but actually transforming the talk into action. My friend and mentor Ralph Peterson refers to this process as establishing routines. In his book *Life in a Crowded Place* (1992), he says, "Initially, selecting routines requires judgment, but once they have been decided, the emphasis is on doing them. Practice is necessary to get things well established." Part of the challenge lies in getting to know the class and deciding what daily schedule will best suit their needs. Some typical considerations:

◆ When is the best time to hold class discussions?
◆ How long can a quiet reading period be sustained?
◆ When will it be necessary to include more active work?
◆ What is the best time of day for mathematics?
◆ How can I organize the week to include large blocks of time for special projects?

Establishing a routine takes time. In the beginning it requires many hours of conversation to create and refine the plan. When children are a part of this process, they see their responsibility in making it work. If they have a role in determining how their daily lives are organized, they care more about making sure that everything goes smoothly. For example, when children consistently carried their conflicts from lunch recess into the classroom each day, we decided we needed to establish a ten-minute "playground talk" before starting our afternoon. If I forget about this talk and go ahead with my agenda, one of the children will invariably say, "Uh, Mary, what about 'playground talk'?" The predictability of such a schedule allows children to anticipate what comes next. When they feel a sense of security about their daily school life, they are more able to risk the unknown.

Children will feel safe when they feel they belong. Along with the practice of establishing classroom routines, we must practice learning how to cultivate positive relationships. We have to practice ways to be a good friend so that everyone will feel safely connected to the rest of the community. This happens through ongoing conversations and also through related work with literature. During the first weeks of school, our discussions focus primarily on learning how to care for each other and the classroom environment we inhabit. Before we can concentrate on reading, writing, and mathematics, we need to develop an awareness of those who accompany us on our journey as learners. We need to know who our traveling companions will be, how they live their lives, and how they wish to be treated so that they can best learn. We have to establish a plan for how we will conduct ourselves in this complex venture and, in particular, how we will solve some of the complex social issues that we will face.

Literature plays a strong role in the process in that it helps to establish examples of ways to treat each other by providing metaphors for living. One powerful metaphor came to us from a book we read one morning, and again on several occasions throughout the year. *Brother Eagle, Sister Sky* (1991) is a book with text based on words attributed to Chief Seattle and beautiful illustrations by Susan Jeffers. I was aware that the book is the subject of some controversy centering on varying opinions about whose words the book actually presents, and we discussed this issue prior to reading the book. However, I chose to read it because the message it contained deeply moved me, and I thought it would be good for the class to hear it. One quote stood out:

> This we know: All things are connected like the blood that unites us.
> We did not weave the web of life,
> We are merely a strand in it.
> Whatever we do to the web, we do to ourselves.

We talked about the meaning of this passage. Bryce commented, "It reminds me of the speech Lincoln gave at Gettysburg. It just had the same feeling. It was just, nice." A few days later, we returned to the book after a conflict between two children had occurred. We had a long talk about how we should treat other people and how if we hurt someone, we hurt everyone. Aaron had a thought about this issue: "Let's just say that life is like a forest. Every time you treat somebody badly, it's like cutting down another tree."

Aaron's metaphor about the forest was a starting point for our blueprint. It remained a strong reminder throughout the year of our place in the web of life, of which we are all a part. It helped us establish some basic and important ground rules for how to treat each other. When incidents arose, such as excluding others from playground games, the metaphor helped us get back on track. As one child said, "Maybe we need to think about planting trees instead of cutting them down."

An important part of establishing routines and developing a strong sense of community at the beginning of the year involves learning to know the people around us. When we do this, we come to appreciate what they can teach us about ourselves and the world. This process occurs through stories people tell, projects they make, and interests they share. We learn who we can turn to for specific questions or help. Children and teachers quickly realize who is a whiz on certain computer programs and who knows how to draw horses. We also recognize what we can bring to others. As we begin to glimpse the strengths, interests, and expertise each person brings to our classroom life, we are able to find our place in the larger community. Sometimes this happens in individual ways; at other times, it happens collaboratively. More often than not, the two processes occur simultaneously.

When learners work this way, a sense of freedom and confidence permeates the classroom environment. Although the teacher maintains the role of guide and mentor, children are not completely dependent on the teacher to tell them what to do and what or how they should learn. Students will pursue their own ideas and seek knowledge because of a personal interest. In other words, they have the confidence to make their own curriculum.

Some may read this scenario and visualize chaos. How can a classroom exist when all of its inhabitants are doing something different at the same time? I will be the first to admit that it's not a neat and tidy way to teach. A teacher who works this way has to be able to pay attention to many activities occurring simultaneously. Someone is always asking for my help, and I've had to get used to hearing my name called frequently. I have also learned to delegate responsibilities. For example, one child has mastered the CD-ROM encyclopedia, so I send others who need information to her. If I've noticed a child recently studying a book another child could benefit from, I suggest they work together for awhile.

Spending time at the beginning of the year laying the foundation for our life together as learners has allowed me to organize my classroom so that many kinds of learning can occur simultaneously. Once the initial blueprint is established, we can move into larger, more inclusive content studies which serve as a broad base from which learners work. Within the studies, children can pursue their individual interests. If a child's interest doesn't tie into the larger study, he or she is encouraged to do an independent study or wait until a class study can be undertaken in which it will be included.

In establishing content studies, I always attempt to keep the work as integrated as possible. That is, I make every effort to include as many subject areas as I can. I try to provide opportunities for the children to do research, to write, to express their knowledge artistically, and to share their learning with an audience. The focus of each study will determine whether or not the content is science or social science, mathematics, art, or a combination of several of these.

What follows is a description of several studies which have evolved in my classroom. Each study has started from a different point of inspiration, and each has manifested in a slightly different way. This happens according to the nature of each class, each topic, and each child's way of expressing knowledge. These studies are not presented as recipes to be duplicated. Instead, I offer them as possibilities for other teachers to consider in their own process of handcrafting a classroom curriculum, and as a means for thinking of content development in a new way.

Magic in the Making

I was always busy as a child—busy with projects and play that were self-directed. I spent very little time in front of the television, and my mother refused to buy us coloring books. We had chores and a few scheduled activities, but for the most part my siblings and I were left to our own resources for entertainment. There was always time to play. Especially during the winter months, I spent a fair amount of time at my dad's workbench in the basement. It was there I made doll furniture, skateboards, and other constructed items. When I was seven, my mother introduced me to her sewing machine. Although I resisted her efforts to make me sew a straight stitch and tear zippers out if they were bunched up, I'm glad now that I had such a perfectionist as a teacher. The early training I received expanded the possibilities for what I could create with my hands—and in my own child way, it helped me make sense of my world as I attempted to re-create what was around me.

In my classroom I have always made sure my students have these same opportunities. As with anything, the use of projects and handwork has evolved over time. We have always used artwork for expressive purposes, but the projects have become something slightly different. Projects generally begin with an idea and are often used to examine or explore that idea. They are always self-directed and often take many weeks to complete. Some are never completed because they undergo transformations into something else. My students eagerly look forward to projects.

Each Friday afternoon the children in my class drag out the fabric, wood, glue, paper towel tubes, lots of tape, blocks, paper, and other assorted materials. To realize their creations, they learn to operate a sewing machine, stitch with thread and needles, and safely handle tools such as saws, drills, and hammers. I become less of a teacher and more of an assistant. Sometimes I become the troubleshooter—rethreading the sewing machine, changing drill bits, and adjusting the printer. As much as possible, I try to stay out of the way and just observe.

One Friday I noticed that Kristin seemed to be in a mood in which she needed her own space. Her way of creating that space was to barricade off a small area with pillows near my desk. She sat there away from everyone else and drew. Nobody bothered her, and it seemed to be a constructive way to solve her need for private space. I found out later that she was also making a birthday card for someone in the room, and she didn't want the person to see her making it.

Nearby, Robert and Bryce were involved with the blocks, making a tall stacked structure. At one point Robert exclaimed, "Look, we're making a human body, and this is the spine!" It *did* resemble a spine. They made the tower about five feet high and, unfortunately, right as we were going to photograph it, it fell over. I was pleased to note the variety of structures these children built.

Dress-ups were a big draw, especially for the most social girls. I noticed that Michele didn't enter the dress-up play directly, but she liked to put on the long white skirt as she did something else. It was wonderful to see her (in the dress-up skirt) with Michael at the woodworking table. He carefully and gently took the time to explain to her how to use the drill. As he explained, he leaned over slightly so she could hear him. It was a tender moment that revealed his care and concern for her. Michael could usually be found in the woodworking area. His strength was there, and he always used the tools carefully to complete his projects.

Woodworking was quite popular with other children as well. Some stayed with wood for several hours, while others, like Aaron, completed their work quickly and then moved to the paints for finishing touches. I observed him getting out the paints, which he generously poured into containers. He had red, green, orange, and black, but he mostly painted his wooden artifact black—LOTS of layers' worth. He was pleased with himself and announced, "Did you know that you can cut rectangles out of cloth to carry painted things so you won't get paint on your hands?" He had used his creativity not only to make his project but also to design and implement a functional apparatus for moving his freshly painted creation.

In another part of the room, Brandon was busy with hand sewing. He made a delightful green leather pillow for his stuffed tiger. He spent a long time carefully sewing it up and stuffing it. His workmanship was impressive. Meanwhile, Deanna and Margaret drew with stencils at a nearby table. They worked with unbelievable concentration at this activity, which they chose nearly every week. They seemed to enjoy the precision and control of the colored pencils with stencils.

Jeff, Richard, and Nicholas worked together with the leather, paper towel tubes, yarn, and cloth. They made some clothes for stuffed animals and later worked with the wood to make a rather fancy birdhouse. Later, when Jacob had a problem trying to figure out a way to attach a top piece over the cockpit of the plane he was building, Jeff exclaimed, "If only we had hinges!" I made a mental note to show them how to make a hinge with leather and tiny nails the next week.

Project day is such an exciting time for all of us. It is a concrete example of what we do all year with learning: we take ordinary things around us and transform them into surprising and wonderful creations. It is a day full of serious work, delightful play, and collaboration, often between unlikely pairs. Strengths of children surface in ways that are very different from those in our work during the rest of the week.

For some of the children, projects offer an opportunity to gain membership in our classroom community. When Michele asked to make a pillow with the sewing machine, I helped her sew it. She did a fine job of operating the machine. She stuffed the pillow carefully with old scraps of cloth and, with minimal help, stitched it closed. When it was finished, she shared her pillow with the class, grinning from ear to ear as she described how she made it. She had found her niche in our class. In the weeks following Michele's first pillow creation, numerous children sought her out to help them make pillows. Some asked her outright to make a pillow for them. It was quite a breakthrough at the end of one project day when Michele sat in a chair in front of the class and announced, "I want everybody to stop asking me to make them pillows." When I asked her to elaborate on her comment, she explained that she didn't mind *helping* people make their pillows, but she didn't have time to actually *make* pillows for them. What struck me about this episode was not only Michele's elevated role as our class pillow expert, but also her elevated confidence in herself. Having acquired the skills necessary to make something others valued and wanted for themselves, Michele came to view herself more favorably as a person. She could do something others wanted to be able to do as well. Knowing that others sought her expertise gave her the courage to publicly acknowledge her appreciation for their respect—and at the same time explain that she couldn't do others' work for them because she had her own important work to do.

What I observe during projects often tells me more about a child than anything else he or she does. I find out who likes solitude and who can work well with others. I notice that some children always choose to work alone, even when asked by others to join them. Their work seems to be more important to them than the opportunity to socialize. I take note of who needs help thinking of a project idea. Some children seem to have a plan each week and get right to work. Others regularly can't decide what to do and need an idea from me to get started. Some seem to do better when they have fewer choices rather than more. I observe differences in the number of projects some children do. A few do many quick projects in one afternoon, and others seem to be able to sustain interest in an ongoing project over several weeks. This shows me the degree to which a child is committed to his or her work and how much passion is felt for a certain project. I notice this level of interest varies from child to child on different projects. A child may sustain interest in this way with one project and not another. Providing the opportunity to explore a variety of projects seems to be essential for all children to experience a deeper commitment to a project at one time or another. Occasionally, this commitment will occur in conjunction with a larger class study. And sometimes the projects help us find our way to answers to difficult questions. This happened the year that Magic Johnson announced he was retiring from professional basketball.

When Earvin "Magic" Johnson, the great Lakers star, told the world he was retiring because he was infected with the HIV virus, I knew my class would have many questions. I expected that the many sports enthusiasts in our class would want to know how he got HIV, what it was, and why he would no longer be playing in the NBA.

Magic's news affected us all. For some, it brought a feeling of sadness that the career of someone so talented was apparently coming to an end. For others, there was new awareness of a disease that is both scary and mysterious. I felt pressure to discuss with seven- and eight-year-olds issues which have previously been delayed until later in their lives. I wanted to give them honest information without saying too much or telling them something that might confuse or frighten them. AIDS and HIV infection were topics that I knew must be addressed skillfully. Our school has no set curriculum, and I realized I'd have to design a study specific to my group of students. I encouraged the children to talk to their parents about their questions as I gathered resources and struggled with these questions:

◆ How much should children know about worldly issues that are life-threatening or potentially so?

◆ How can I be honest yet withhold information that could be frightening to them?

◆ As a teacher, how can I address the varying degrees of information children bring to my classroom?

◆ What are the best ways to help children grow up to be good decision makers so that they can make informed choices as they reach maturity?

I struggled between wanting to preserve the innocence of childhood and needing to respond to the demands of our times. The material necessary for such a study was not only abstract and beyond the children cognitively, but was outside the realm of what I believed was appropriate for young children. I had to think of a way to make it fit their developmental needs and at the same time offer a concrete way to begin answering some of their questions. I decided to approach the study of AIDS within the context of a study of the entire human body. We began the study as we do most studies we start from scratch: with the children's questions. Here are some of them:

- What kind of surgery do you have to have to get a sperm?
- How do people get headaches?
- How deep is your skin?
- How does the sperm get out of the man's body and into the lady's body?
- Why are babies wrinkled when they're born?
- What's in your brain that makes you think?
- What makes you ticklish?
- How fast does your breath go when you sneeze?
- Why do my eyes have to be watery?
- How can your voice come out?
- How do people get tired?
- What makes you get the flu?
- What part of the body makes you get addicted to things?
- What is AIDS?
- How do you die?

We organized the questions around the different body systems. For example, questions about getting the flu and AIDS were generally categorized under the immune system. Then each child chose the system he or she wanted to investigate further. I suggested that they should choose their system based on interest, rather than because they wanted to work with their closest friends. Most of the children were quite agreeable during this selection process, and everyone was relatively happy with his or her system. The research teams quickly began asking questions and collecting facts. Library books provided some of the stimulus for questions—as did other circumstances around the school. When one of the three-year-olds brought her newborn baby brother into our room for his first visit, Kristin exclaimed, "So that's why her mom had a big tummy! I was longing to ask her about that!"

As the study evolved, the work moved in several directions. First, there were the daily conversations between children that let me know the extent to which they were committed to the study. They talked about it throughout the day. It was fascinating to notice how the children pooled information to help each other along. One day Nicole kept asking Richard about the brain. She'd ask, "How many systems are there in the brain?" Richard replied, "You mean parts?" Without missing a beat he turned to Aaron and inquired, "Aaron, how do you spell esophagus?" Their informal conversations revealed not only the children's questions and interests, but also the connections they were making between learning experiences. When Margaret and Michele sat on the floor working on their research of the skin with Laura, our student teacher, I heard Laura trying to explain about fingerprints. She said, "When they put people in jail, they take their fingerprints." Margaret paused for a moment and replied, "Like Rosa Parks." I was taken aback by Margaret's comment because during all the time we'd studied the Civil Rights Movement and Rosa Parks's life, I had wondered how much Margaret understood. Her interests had seemed to lie elsewhere. Her comment about Rosa Parks and jail told me that she had not only listened but had also understood more than I'd thought.

Other conversations with the whole class demonstrated a similar blending of concepts and ideas. After a visit to the nursing home, seven-year-old Laura said, "There was a lady at the nursing home who had a yellow face. It gave me a sign and reminded me of Stefanie's aunt [who had recently died of some sort of liver complication]." I asked if this reminded them of anyone else, and Brandon said it reminded him of Mary in *The Secret Garden* (who was jaundiced before she started getting fresh air and a healthier life). Somebody asked, "What causes your face to be yellow?" I replied, "It has something to do with the liver." I suggested that the digestive system group might want to pursue this further. Michele added, "It has to do with the skin, too, because your skin turns yellow!"

As conversations about the human body abounded in our room, children were engaged in a considerable amount of writing and reading. Their ultimate goal was to gather enough information to be able to make a presentation to the class about their body system. Each child had a research notebook consisting of a question page and separate pages for taking notes on relevant facts. They wrote their questions first and answered them as the information appeared in their research.

The emphasis was on making the children so familiar with facts and the related terminology of their system that they would feel comfortable talking about their system in front of the class. Throughout the study I kept emphasizing the idea that we were scientists and reminding them that the information needed to be presented scientifically. This attitude was particularly helpful for the children who had to present information that might evoke a silly or embarrassing response. One of the primary reasons for pursuing the study was to help the children be comfortable and aware of information about their bodies.

Robert and Aaron did an exemplary job of presenting the digestive system to the class. They prepared notes, transparencies, and models of the digestive system to help explain what they'd learned. They displayed their first transparency and began explaining about the saliva glands. They moved on to the stomach and said, "It has acid that turns your food into mush." Progressing through the system on to the intestines, Robert said, "The intestines sort out the good stuff and the bad stuff." He further explained that the bad stuff turns into a bowel movement and the good stuff goes to the blood. Jeff fielded a question from the audience: "After it [digestion] happens, do you grow a little?"

Aaron replied, "No, that's the endocrine system." Without missing a beat, he resumed his presentation, adding, "You need saliva or it would be uncomfortable to get food down without it." Aaron then proceeded to describe the esophagus by saying, "Some air clears up the esophagus. A little goes down the esophagus. If you didn't have your esophagus your food would go every which way."

Robert redirected the presentation back to the intestines. He said, "If the small intestine was flattened out, it would be the size of two tennis courts." The appendix was mentioned, and then Aaron asked, "Remember when we studied France last year? Remember that *Madeline* book we read about the appendix? It [the appendix] doesn't have any use in the body."

Aaron and Robert continued with their description of the digestive system for nearly an hour. After completing their presentation, they took questions from their classmates. They discussed such issues as why we get stomachaches, why the feces have lines in them, and why we throw up. Aaron explained, "How you throw up is when your food doesn't have time to digest, it doesn't go down, it goes up." He elaborated by saying that this usually happens when you do something active right after eating. When asked about when someone vomits during the night when they've been sleeping, Aaron responded with, "Maybe you've been moving around in your bed too much at night!"

As each team of experts took a turn presenting its information to the class, I found that each presentation was not only packed full of interesting facts, but also contained a twist of personal interpretation by each set of presenters. For example, when Richard and Bryce gave their talk about the brain and nervous system, they explained what happens when you stumble: "When you stumble, your brain gets tangled up with other parts of your body. Like if you're talking, your brain forgets about your walking." When Jason gave his presentation about the eye and ear, one of the children asked him what makes ear wax. He thought about it a moment and replied,

"It's like your ear puking." When asked to elaborate, he explained that the wax produced is the ear's way of fending off unwanted substances in the ear.

The other children appreciated the personal touches each child added to the presentations. After Deanna finished her talk about the urinary system, which included a large clay model of the kidney, Shannon said, "You did a really good presentation because I didn't even know what the urinary system is and now I know. That's how I know it was a good presentation." The personal touches included more than the children's interpretations of information. Like Deanna, Jason made a model of his subject. Jason's model of the eye was made from a clear plastic egg-shaped container attached to a blue light bulb. He added a pupil and iris with tape and lightweight cardboard. When he plugged his model in, it glowed and looked really authentic. Robert's model of the digestive system was an innovative arrangement of tubes and trapdoors. He dropped a piece of popcorn into one tube (esophagus) and then pulled a little trap door. The trap door released a marble that had been covered with masking tape and colored brown to represent the feces. It was a big hit with the audience.

What I noticed about the presentations was the level of confidence with which the children delivered their information. The dialogue between children, as well as the time spent preparing their presentations, gave the children a sense of comfort with the material. Robert and Aaron had no problem discussing bowel movements with their peers. They felt familiar with their information, and it was natural for them to want to share it with everyone else.

Midway through the study, we decided we should collect the information and put it in written form. It was getting toward the end of the school year, and I knew there wouldn't be sufficient time for the children to go through the lengthy process of writing out all they knew. So, as each group finished its presentation, I met with them at the computer. They talked, and I asked questions and typed. We decided to include one of their transparency drawings with each report.

Robert and Aaron's final report and drawing are shown in Figure 3. Their report exemplifies the extent and depth of knowledge acquired during our study. It is also filled with their own voices and humor. As my fingers scrambled on the keyboard to record the information they had gathered, I was

---

Digestive System
by
Robert and Aaron

The scientific name for the digestive system is the gastrointestinal tract. But we will call it the digestive system. The salivary glands make your saliva. It softens your food when you are chewing. If you did not have saliva it would take you about three minutes to chew something two or three inches thick. Saliva mixes with food and when it goes down into your stomach it mixes with stomach acids and helps digest. Saliva helps the esophagus while the food is going down.

The esophagus is a tube to let your food go down into your stomach. If you did not have an esophagus your food would splatter every which way when you eat. Some of it might, about 5%, go into the stomach. The rest would clog up your systems. Of course, that is why God made the esophagus.

The stomach is like a built-in food processor with no blades, but acids. Your stomach acids turn your food into throw-up. How you get stomach aches is when you eat, the stomach needs oxygen to help digest the food and the blood carries it. But when you exercise right after you eat, you do not get enough blood to digest your food because it goes to other parts of your body. The food sits there too long and you get a stomach ache. When you feel nauseated you better rush to the bathroom and stick your head very close to the toilet. Ask your parents for some yucky smelling medicine and it will make you throw up. Then you'll feel better.

The liver is like a factory. It holds all your nutrients for when you need them. It produces bile. Bile is like a detergent that helps clean out fats in your digestive system. Have you ever eaten a greasy food and then put the plate under cold water? Did you find out that it would not come off without soap? If you did, the soap is just like bile but without soap.

The small intestines sort out your food for the parts that you need and the parts that you don't need. The parts that you need go back into your bloodstream. The parts that you don't need get turned into stuff that looks like diarrhea. Then it goes into the large intestine that filters the water out and turns it into regular looking bowel movement. It will go to the rectum and when you start to feel it, it means you better rush to the toilet. The anus is your bottom opening and that is where the bowel movement comes out. Without the digestive system you would die because all the other systems would get clogged up.

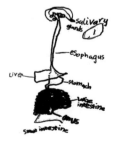

Figure 3   Robert and Aaron's report on the digestive system.

again amazed at how much they had learned. Seeing the collection of system summaries accumulate reminded me how
complex and extensive this work had become.

Although the children were assembling a wealth of
information and beginning to share it with others, I wasn't
certain how much they were really understanding. The information was abstract and complicated. I wanted to think of a
way to help them understand better, a way which would also
enable me to assess what they really knew. I thought of their
project work and how it frequently lets me see what a child is
thinking. One day I suggested that they each make a
three-dimensional model of the human body, combining their
handcrafting skills with their new knowledge of the human
body. The results were even more fascinating than the presentations they had made to the class. Furthermore, as the presentations were made, the models became more detailed as
the children incorporated the new information.

I first showed them a videotape of a previous student's
human body model made with paper sacks, ribbons, balloons, and other miscellaneous materials. The video inspired
them to build their own models. They quickly pulled out
cardboard boxes, tubes, yarn, marbles, paper plates, styrofoam, and a myriad of other items. They all began in different
ways. Some of the children began by drawing. Others
jumped right into the three-dimensional work. Regardless of
their means of expression, their models and the related conversations that arose showed me more specifically what the
children had come to know. As I looked around the room
while this process went on, they reminded me of a group of
surgeons busy with the task of making people whole.

Jeff and Nicholas were two of the most enthusiastic students. I watched them one day as they hovered over their projects. Each had his own model going, but they took turns working on each other's. On this particular day they were adding
the next detail to Jeff's model of the human body, a fetus in its
amniotic sac. They used a balloon for the baby, drawing facial
features with a marker. They decided to make the sac out of a
clear plastic cup filled with water and tightly sealed.

While they were working, I moved slightly to observe what Aaron and Robert were doing. I asked Aaron a question, addressing him by his first name. He said, "It's Drs. Janney, Schwimmer, Hushek, and Smith. Please call us by our doctor names!" Without pause he looked at Nicholas and asked, "Hey, where are his testicles?"

Nicholas replied, "You mean ovaries! It's a woman!" Then Robert, who had been concentrating on assembling his model exclaimed, "Yo, doctors, it works!"

It was fascinating to see how the ideas of one child influenced the work of others. When Brandon came up with the idea of making a rib cage out of paper plates, we immediately saw different versions of his idea in other children's models. Nicholas and Jeff worked so closely it was hard to know which of them came up with the idea for the moving knee joints and Styrofoam toes on Nicholas's model. When we heard the presentation on the respiratory system, they immediately went to work devising lungs that would expand and contract. They ended up using balloons inserted through openings in their models through which they could blow to simulate air filling up the lung. Nicholas added an extra touch by painting one balloon black—to represent a smoker's lung.

As each group made its oral presentation, the models became more elaborate. Nicholas's model's head had eyeballs, a brain made of colored tissue paper, and a pituitary gland. He attached egg carton pieces connected with yarn down the middle for the vertebrae and spinal cord. Like Jeff's, his model had paper towel tubes for arms with veins and arteries appearing through the cut-out windows. Nicholas's model was different from the others in that it was actually shaped like a human being. The chest area was made up of a series of flaps which included muscles made of red cloth; the lungs, of course; the digestive system with a paper-tube esophagus; and red construction paper blood cells glued all over the inside.

The model construction process gave me an opportunity to see what kind of information they had internalized. It was related to, but different from, the information they'd gathered through their reading and research. As I listened to them discuss how to put what they knew about the human body into a concrete form, I could almost see their thought processes in action. Overhearing them negotiate how parts should be assembled or adapted gave me a visible means of knowing how they interpreted what they'd learned.

It was equally fascinating to listen to them explain their models to visitors who came to our classroom. Richard captivated one guest with his lengthy description of how the brain sends messages to different parts of the body. To demonstrate his point, he took a marble and inserted it in the head of his model. It rolled from the brain down through a series of tubes and out the end of the arm. He explained that when you hurt yourself the brain sends out the message, and it travels along the nerves to where you're hurt. When the message gets there, "you cry or something."

As I observed the children making their models and sharing them with others, I gained new insights. The process gave me a new kind of awareness as a teacher:

◆ It's not enough to give children information. They need opportunities to talk about their ideas and the content of a study. They develop a greater understanding of the material when they have a chance to share their ideas and bounce them off of each other. Oftentimes another child can make a concept more clear to a child than an adult can.

◆ Hearing the questions of other children is important. When one child asks a question, he or she not only learns that it's acceptable to ask about things, but also gives others ideas for their own questions. This in turn broadens a child's understanding as more questions are answered.

◆ It's necessary to provide opportunities to celebrate what children are learning all the way through the course of a study. Seeing and hearing what other children are discovering opens up possibilities for others. This celebration of learning also gives children ideas about where to look for information, how to go about finding it, and how to organize it in written form. A more involved celebration time can be included at the end of a study.

◆ Children need ways to express what they have learned beyond reading and writing about it. This is true for all children and especially for those who may be more vulnerable in these areas. Particularly when material is abstract, children benefit from opportunities to create concrete representations.

◆ When children are involved in making concrete representations of something they've learned, they work hard to be sure that their creations are accurate. They seek opinions of others, ask for ideas, and give feedback. The classroom organization needs to include time for this process to occur. The environment also needs to be one in which children feel safe to try out their ideas, confident that they will not be criticized by others.

◆ Other classroom activities can influence the outcome of projects such as models of the human body. I saw a direct link between the body models and the block building, marble-rolling structures made of tubes, and other projects children selected throughout the year. They quickly applied techniques they'd mastered in earlier projects. Richard's model with the marble for brain messages was a good example.

◆ Children periodically need to share the process of making a project. Some of the most exciting ideas children have are inspired by something they've seen another child do. This sharing can occur within the class or with visitors from the outside. Through explaining a process, a child often realizes more clearly what he or she has learned and additionally may discover the answer to a problem he or she has been trying to solve with the model.

◆ Children need time to develop ideas, especially when they are expressing them in written or concrete form. Work can be extensive only when it has had time to grow.

As our study drew to a close, I noticed that, in addition to the wonderful conversations and models that filled our classroom, the children's writing contained more and more of their newly acquired information about the human body. One day Richard casually walked over and handed me his journal. He had provided a detailed response to my question the previous day about the gender of his human body model. His response is shown in Figure 4. What impressed me about Richard's writing was the level at which he had internalized the information and taken it on as his own. He was matter-of-fact in his approach to his work and had confidence in what he knew. He understood, with his eight-year-old's mind, the difference between the male and female body and had no

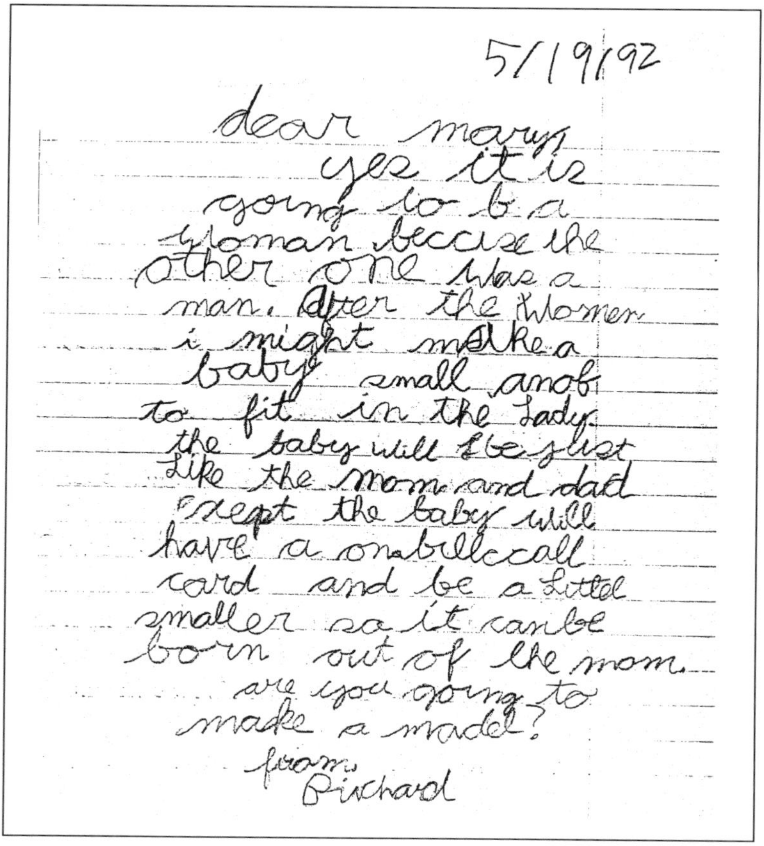
5/19/92
dear mary
yes it is
going to b a
woman becuse the
other one was a
man. after the women
i might make a
baby small anof
to fit in the lady.
the baby will be just
like the mom and dad
exept the baby will
have a onabillcall
card and be a little
smaller so it can be
born out of the mom.
are you going to
make a model?
from
Richard

A note from Richard explaining his decision to build a female human body model. Figure 4

trouble explaining to me what he knew. Furthermore, he realized that in order to accurately depict a pregnant woman with his model, he had to make the baby similar but smaller to fit inside the mother. He knew the baby needed an umbilical cord to survive before it was born. I noticed that, like Richard, many of the children had reached a new level of familiarity and understanding of the details of the human body.

I could tell how confident Robert, Aaron, and Jeff felt with their new-found knowledge when they decided to write a manual called *How to Make a Human Body*. It began with this introduction: "These are suggestions to make a box into a human body because we thought it would be a good project." The book includes diagrams of the various body systems and lists the materials one might need to represent them in a model. Figure 5 shows two of their pages.

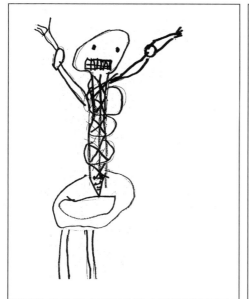

Figure 5   Two pages from *How to Make a Human Body* by Robert, Aaron, and Jeff. Their text reads: "Skeletal system/Styrofoam/to make the skeleton/you need toilet paper rolls and white paper. Stapler."

Ironically, AIDS and the HIV virus—which started our human body study in the first place—were the most difficult topics to talk about and understand, not because of the subject matter per se, but because the immune system is so abstract and thus hard to represent. We could talk about it, but it was difficult to make a model of the immune system. Shannon did as good a job of explaining it as one could expect from an eight-year-old. She included many facts and at the same time included her own interpretations. For example, she ended her presentation by assuring the class that "Magic's blood is not running AIDS *yet!*" Her final report and illustration are shown in Figure 6.

As Shannon stood before the class giving her report on the immune system, the final one of our study, I realized how far we'd come since the day we first discussed Magic Johnson's

The immune system is in the blood. You cannot see it but the immune system has a nickname. It is white blood cells. Also you have red blood cells. Your red blood cells float in a river in your veins. Your white blood cells float with the red blood cells.

The white blood cells are not exactly like red blood cells because the white blood cells are the immune system. They float with your red blood cells and all over your body. They protect your body from diseases.

AIDS is a disease that attacks the white blood cells. If you don't have your white blood cells and then you get a cold, you can die. These are some ways to get AIDS:

1. If you have sexual contact with somebody with AIDS you can get it.

2. If you share a needle with somebody with AIDS.

3. If somebody has a cut and the other person has a cut and they contact blood and one of them has AIDS that person can get AIDS.

4. If you share blood products with somebody with AIDS you can get it.

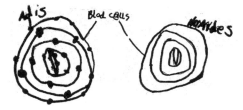

Shannon's report on the immune system. Figure 6

announcement. The children's conversations, models, questions, and reports all served as records of this growth process.
They demonstrated how far an interest can carry children
along, even when the subject matter is difficult and complex.
Their work also showed me that children will meet a subject
head-on if given the opportunity and will seek multiple ways of
expressing what they know. And more important, the study
demonstrated how essential it is for children to use their hands
to make things that will help them understand what they are
learning.

One visitor to our class questioned whether the children
were really grasping any of the information. He thought they
weren't understanding, just repeating back things they'd
heard. My response to his doubts is this: The children will
obviously process the information given to them differently
than adults would. They will take it in and make it their own
in a way that fits where they are developmentally. As they
grow older—after having had an opportunity to construct
models, talk with others, and research the information in an
appealing way—they will reconstruct their knowledge again
and again. Even if the nervous system is an abstract concept
for an eight-year-old to grasp, she will benefit more from having played around with marbles, dropping them down a
paper tube to represent messages being sent from the brain,
than from not having had the chance at all. The experiences
my students have had as second graders, using their hands
and minds together to study the human body systems, will
serve as a foundation for future inquiry and more mature
understanding in time. And who knows what fine surgeon's
career might begin with a Styrofoam pelvis constructed inside
a cardboard box? It is here that a teacher's profound responsibility lies, for in giving children new ways to expand their
thinking about themselves and their world, we are leaving the
door to the future wide open.

More Than Just a Game

In the corner of my bedroom, there was a built-in cupboard. It was a perfect place for my trolls to live. Especially in the winter when it was so cold outside, I spent hundreds of hours adjusting this private living space for them. My trolls had a large wardrobe of felt clothing, as well as beds (with bedding), a table, a fireplace, and chairs. Some of the furniture was borrowed from my dollhouse, but most of it I made from wood scraps in our basement. At Christmastime the trolls' stockings hung from the mantle of their hand-painted fireplace beside their Christmas tree. So they wouldn't feel left out, I wrapped tiny packages and tucked them under their tree.

Since the trolls and their house were permanent residents of my bedroom, I didn't often take them beyond that space. Having the need for a more portable "family," I found an old sewing basket and turned it into living quarters for an assortment of small rubber eraser animals. These too sported felt clothing, although theirs was much less elaborate than the trolls' because they were so much smaller. The basket housed soft beds that were permanently attached to the floor so they wouldn't tumble around when traveling. There was a wall with a doorway dividing the basket in half to give the animals their own private spaces. Miniature pictures hung on the walls. It was a self-contained world within a world that absorbed my attention as I made adjustments and applied new ideas that came along.

My solitary activities with the basket and the troll homes provided endless hours of creative play that was similar yet different from the play I was involved in with the neighborhood children. It was similar in that it was an ongoing process of revision; time seemed limitless, and there wasn't an ending point imposed by an external person (a grown-up). The play was sustained as long as I wanted it to continue. It was different in that the emphasis was on tiny details, rather than on creating something big and complex with others. It was a private world over which I had complete control. This quiet activity helped to develop my interior world; it mostly existed in my mind, enhanced by the simple props I made with my own hands. I would hope that all children experience this kind of creativity in some way or another, for it is one of the richest memories I have carried with me from childhood.

I have concerns for the many children today who have so little time for such play. After a full day of school, their time outside of school is frequently filled up with many other kinds of activities: piano lessons, enrichment classes, Nintendo, television. When do they have time to develop their interior spaces? The hours I spent playing with my dolls and all their accessories gave me a chance to see that I had within me the power to create a world within a world. Anything was possible. I could make changes that fit new ideas. There was no need to rush or hurry on to the next thing; everything would be waiting for me the next time I returned to that imaginary world. Furthermore, the fact that it was ongoing gave me an opportunity to reflect on what I wanted to do next. The continuity allowed intuition to develop.

The chance to sustain this kind of play has influenced how I think about school today. It has shaped the kinds of activities I present for my students to be involved in as they move through a year with me. While we learn big things together—about the world, about history, about the future—I also try to give them opportunities to manipulate small things. Knowing how full their lives are outside of school, I make an effort to provide them with opportunities to do work in the classroom that is ongoing and continuous, where they can make choices and revise their private thinking.

An example of this ongoing work comes to mind. One summer, during a week-long mini-course on architecture and houses, I presented the idea of making model homes to a group of students. After weeks of collecting wood scraps, discarded tiles, cardboard, small mechanical parts, and anything else of this nature I could get my hands on, I offered the invitation and stepped out of the way. The results were remarkable. Deanna created a multilayer tree house for her miniature trolls that included an elevator to lift them to the upper levels. Her house had beds and terraces with miniature sponge trees and bushes. Even the Swiss Family Robinson would have been envious. Michael constructed an authentic-looking adobe house of boxes, mud, sand, and clay. He took the time to make a ladder of sticks with yarn wrapped around the rungs to hold them in place. He found pictures of different wild animals and placed them appropriately in the grass yard he'd made around his house. Small green and yellow cucumbers from the garden, along with pictures of rock writings glued to the wall near his front door, gave Michael's house a distinctly Southwest touch. Mia's home was the most intricate. It was like a Quonset hut with a removable roof for viewing the interior spaces. Hers was furnished with everything from a swimming pool to spaghetti heaped on tiny handmade dishes. Small clay fixtures were included in the bathroom to give its inhabitants all the comforts of home. The yard—green snips of yarn and retired Easter grass—was enclosed by a straw fence made of wall-covering samples.

The houses as final products were fascinating and intriguing, but the process was even more powerful. Although the course was presented the first week of summer school as a one-week venture, when I returned to the school weeks later—after numerous other topics and projects had been presented—the children were still making houses. They would complete their other activities and then return to the houses. I was astounded until I remembered my work as a child with my trolls and their home. Then I understood what was happening: these children had found a way to sustain the same sort of ongoing play with the houses as their medium. Although the house project was part of a special summer program where the usual amount of time didn't have to be devoted each day to academics, it opened up possibilities for learning activities throughout the school year. The houses reminded me that children need to use their hands to create and manipulate small environments that are theirs alone. And they need time to let such projects develop. A chance to offer this kind of activity arose one year within the context of a study of our environment.

During the first days of the new school year, we began saving the garbage left from our lunches: bottles, cans, wrappers, plastic bags. The garbage collecting was the introduction to our study of the environment, which I had selected as our first class study of the year. One afternoon we sorted out the trash in small groups and came together as a whole group to make a garbage graph. There was disagreement about which category some items—such as juice boxes—should fall into. It was tedious work, and we didn't complete it as planned.

The next day we finished the garbage graph with a great deal of effort. We came up with two main categories, recyclable and nonrecyclable, and identified the various materials such as glass, foil, plastic, etc. We talked about how it helps the environment if you buy Chee-tos in a big bag and use smaller containers. Jeff said, "But the big bags cost more." I tried to explain to him that actually it's cheaper to buy the bigger ones than the smaller ones, but it was a hard concept to get across. I made a mental note to buy some little ones and a big bag and compare weight and price.

The garbage graph gave us a strong starting point for discussions about waste, recycling, and biodegradable materials. We set up boxes in the classroom for recycling plastic, aluminum, tin, glass, and paper. The school custodians noticed immediately the reduction of trash in our room. In addition to the recycling project, we began a graph of how many trees it takes to make all the newspapers in America on just one Sunday. One source said 500,000 trees every week. I photocopied pages with blocks of 1,000 squares each, and the children colored them green. When the blocks were colored and assembled, we were amazed to see what 500,000 tiny squares looked like. We hung the huge graph in the hallway and were pleased to notice how much talk it stimulated among parents and other students.

Word got around the school that we were studying the environment, and Becky, our first-grade teacher, requested that Aaron come down to her class to explain about recycling and our garbage graph. After addressing that subject, he took it upon himself to talk to them about the ozone layer and said, "I can tell you that if our atmosphere deteriorates, we're going to have a really hot time!" He added, "We're trying to save the Earth, but we're also trying to save our future." The passion for our study grew.

Our next step was to make a web to organize our thinking for our study. It helped us sort out the various aspects of the environment into categories. The main categories we came up with were energy, pollution, endangered species and the creatures of the Earth, natural resources, and waste and recycling. The finished web is shown in Figure 7. We talked about natural resources. Aaron said that *we* are natural resources and "If we weren't natural resources, probably all of us would be demolished by now. We are natural resources because we help the Earth stay the way it is and by eating the food so more will grow." Richard added, "If we take care of the Earth, the Earth will take care of us." Laura followed with, "The Earth is another mother. We have two." Once the web was finished, we decided to break the study into four parts, starting with endangered species and natural resources. Eventually each child chose a specific topic he or she was interested in researching further.

Some of the children chose topics in which they'd had a previous interest. Although some children had studied their topics before, they wanted to build on previous knowledge. Aaron began his volcano research with a story about a trip he and his family took to Sunset Crater, an extinct volcano in northern Arizona. He sat at the computer and as he typed said, "I'm almost finished! How do you spell *light?*" I suggested that

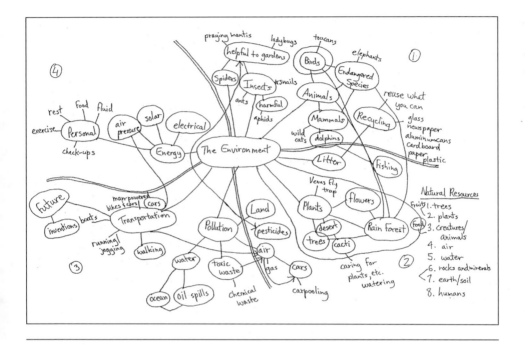

Figure 7   A topic web on the environment, generated after class discussion.

he use his dictionary. He opted for a more convenient route
and called to Bryce who was under a nearby table, "Hey,
Bryce, how do you spell *light?*" Bryce, our ace speller, gave
him the correct spelling, and Aaron moved on to a new train
of thought. He said, "Can you believe I finished my story?" I
replied, "You're fast!" Aaron said, "Yes, I take after my dad!"
Later, after he had time to think some more, he added, "You
know when Sunset Crater blew? I wonder where the top went.
I stayed up all night thinking about what I'm going to type on
my story. I'm always staying up about something. Something in
the future, something about the past . . . always something."

Meanwhile, Jacob was recording information from the
encyclopedia. He had written almost a page of data in his
daily writing book about killer whales. He approached me
with a sheepish grin on his face and asked, "Mary, did you

know that if we had a stomach the size of a killer whale, we could eat a thousand hamburgers at one time?" I asked him to share this information when it was time for author sharing. He was pleased with his work and eager to show his daily writing book to his classmates. I thought to myself how amazing it was that, even with their limited ability as readers, they were able to gather so much information.

Breakthroughs for individual learners began to happen more frequently. Children like Aaron and Jacob were inspired daily to extend themselves as readers and writers. Our study of the environment facilitated this process. Concepts that had eluded children began to have meaning. As we talked more about environmental issues and as children shared resources, terms like recycle, biodegradable, natural resources, and endangered species became part of our everyday vocabulary.

As with our study of the human body, the children also served as resources for each other, delivering information to those who needed it. When Margaret struggled to find information she needed about otters, Liz was right there to assist her. The children discovered multiple resources for information. Jason and Brandon used *As Dead as a Dodo* (Rice 1981) to find out about extinct species and then extended their knowledge by using the globe and various maps to find out where the extinct animals had lived. Richard and Jeff, studying trees, used *The Lorax* to get ideas for tree-cutting machines. Other children spontaneously made smaller webs to organize their information, such as the one by Stefanie and Shannon about water pollution, shown in Figure 8.

There was considerable enthusiasm for working out story problems that arose from reading and general discussions. It was exciting to try to figure out the connection between real-life situations and numbers on the chalkboard. During a conference with Libby and Nicole about polar bears, they told me that polar bears can have one thousand babies in a lifetime. We researched this further and discovered that polar bears actually only live to be thirty-three years old and usually have twin cubs each year. I asked them if they'd like to present this problem to the whole class to figure out how many cubs a polar bear could have in a lifetime. They thought it was a good idea. Without taking into consideration the time it would take for a polar bear to reach reproductive maturity, some of the children arrived at the number sixty-six. Some had multiplied and others added. Other questions were posed: How many years would it take for a polar bear to have one thousand cubs? And how about if they had four cubs a year instead of two? How many years would it take to make one thousand? When we finished, after an hour of intensive work, Aaron exclaimed, "I think we've outdone ourselves for one day!" But just when we thought we'd done the best we could, surprising breakthroughs occurred.

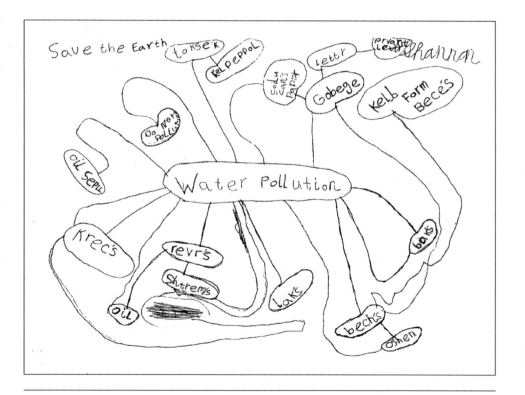

Figure 8   Shannon and Stefanie's topic web on water pollution. Their topics include "beaches," "oil spill," "rivers," "ocean," "toxic," and "garbage."

One morning we arrived in our room and found a note on the chalkboard from Pam, one of the school custodians. It was her third note to the class. The first one congratulated us on our reduction of trash, and the second was about forgetting to put our chairs up (we were too busy thinking about trash!). The note said:

> You guys would make great biospherians! (Hardly any trash)
> Keep up the good work.
>
> Pam

Pam's note reminded us of our personal connection with environmental issues. Fascinated by recent news about the sealing up of Biosphere 2 in nearby Tucson, we stayed in touch with the latest information through newspaper clippings and local TV newscasts. Learning about Biosphere 2 gave us insight into our relationship with Biosphere 1, the Earth. It broadened our awareness of the interconnectedness of all life-forms and the impact one system has upon another.

One day we decided to walk around the neighborhood to explore the various businesses and light industry in the area. Our favorite spot was the construction site at the dairy plant. On our way back to school, we peeked into a garage where a group of mechanics were taking a smoking break. Several children made comments about polluting the air, and then one of them noticed two rather grimy barrels of discarded motor oil behind the building. The children peered into it and started yelling, "Toxic waste! Toxic waste!" I had the feeling we were training a whole new generation of environmental detectives.

The increased environmental awareness in our classroom raised issues similar to those that came up in discussions of AIDS and related topics. Some of the information, such as articles about the deteriorating ozone layer, was frightening to a few of the children. This fear was compounded when several of the children embellished their descriptions of these problems. One of the biggest difficulties I noticed with providing children such information was that it overwhelmed them and made them feel as if they had no control over their environment. We took this opportunity to talk things through and balance out information with the need for feeling safe. I tried to remind them that some of these problems are beyond what we can do personally, but there are many things we can do, such as recycling. I also wanted to give them an opportunity to take what they were learning and apply it to a situation where they *could* have complete control. The chance to do this came when I invited the children to create their own board games using the information collected in their research.

The idea of having children make board games had fascinated me for some time. Kathryn Castle's research (1990) inspired me to try having my students make games a few years ago. But I had never tried incorporating social science or science concepts. This seemed like an opportune time to attempt such work. Once the idea was presented to the children, they took off with it.

Like the human body models, the games provided a way for the children to integrate multiple disciplines to express their knowledge. But the games also allowed them to make something that they could manipulate, and of which they could completely determine the outcome. They could make up the rules and decide who would win or lose. The games also revealed many things about the children themselves and how they worked with others.

One day I observed Richard and Jeff having a disagreement about how they would make their game. Jeff wanted to make separate games, and Richard wanted to make one together. I suggested that they might want to make the same game but each make his own version of it. This seemed to satisfy them, and they continued with their paper drafts, which eventually were used as a guide for their final game board. Their subject was trees, and they decided on a game board design resembling Monopoly. They said, "It's sort of like a tour in a forest with questions. If you get the correct answer, you get the right to go again." They thought of using contact-papered leaves for markers. They were also planning to include tree houses in their game.

When it was time to share work for the day, Richard and Jeff explained their game concept to the class. Robert said, "I think you should use money in your game to save the rain forest." This led to a whole discussion about purchasing land in the rain forest. Several of the children were interested in doing this and asked how the land is protected. Richard said, "There are rangers who watch the rain forest so nobody destroys it." I mentioned to Deanna and Steffen that they might want to use this idea of the rangers in their game about the rain forest. They said they'd think about it.

The children's games showed a marvelous variety. There was Richard and Jeff's game about the forest, and Nicole and Libby's about polar bears. Aaron's game about volcanoes was complex, incorporating information about Sunset Crater, Mount Olympus, Mount Saint Helens, and Kiluea in Hawaii. Players had four lives available in the event of unexpected tragedies. When Shannon heard this she suggested, "If one player dies in the game, another person could continue playing the game so players can learn all the information in the game." Nicholas, who was assisting Aaron, responded, "We're planning on having people play in teams so this can happen." Aaron added that players had a chance to obtain extra life cards in the game.

One of the most impressive aspects of the games was the enthusiasm for the work and the growing camaraderie between children. It was intriguing to observe how they drew on each other for suggestions and ideas in much the same way they did while working on the body models. Likewise, their continuous revision of ideas for their games brought many unimaginable surprises.

One morning, amidst rich dialogue focused on the games, I noticed two boys at a table carefully examining their rulers, making sure they used them precisely to measure the squares they needed for their game boards. I checked in with Nicole and Libby to help them organize their information. I suggested they put their information in little boxes in their daily writing books. I was pleased to note that Margaret was starting to get the concept of making a game. She was beginning to add information from her research to the squares on her board, such as "Otter stops to play with apple." I turned and noticed Jason and Brandon hard at work on the floor. They had come up with an ingenious way to make a large hard surface under their game board—put four clipboards together!

The games about the rain forest led us to further reading and related activities as a whole class. One afternoon we read about the rain forest and how it is being burned and cut down to raise cattle for beef. We briefly discussed the carbon dioxide problem and then talked about erosion. It was a difficult concept to grasp just through talk, so we gathered up a bunch of popsicle sticks and some grey tubs and headed outside to the sand pile. I asked the children to fill up their tubs with sand and then posed the following questions:

◆ What happens when you tilt your tub and pour water over the sand?

◆ How is it different if you stand the popsicle sticks up in the sand?

For the next hour children tried out different things related to the questions and then set up their own experiments. When we were finished, they wrote about the experience. Shannon's entry is shown in Figure 9. Experiences such as this one focusing on the concept of erosion gave the children new knowledge as they returned to their games. They also began to realize that a blending of disciplines could strengthen their understanding of the concepts with which they were working.

As work on the games proceeded, I began to notice a change in the way the children approached their research. I saw that they combined disciplines more frequently. It became more difficult to see where science or social studies ended and writing or math began. For example, Michael approached me one day after reading about whales during silent reading. He said he had a math problem for me. He read that the ocean is 35,840 feet deep and wondered how many blue whales that would be stacked end to end. I asked him how long a blue whale is, and he ran over to get Jacob to find out, since Jacob was one of the whale experts in the class. They decided to save the problem for the whole class to figure out later on. This way of making connections between academic domains was more visible with the games than in any other work we'd done so far. I think this was due primarily to the nature of the activity and the multiple skills required simultaneously to complete the project. In addition to all of the mathematical thinking and problem solving involved in the games, reading and writing, drawing, planning, designing, and rule making were also necessary. At times during the

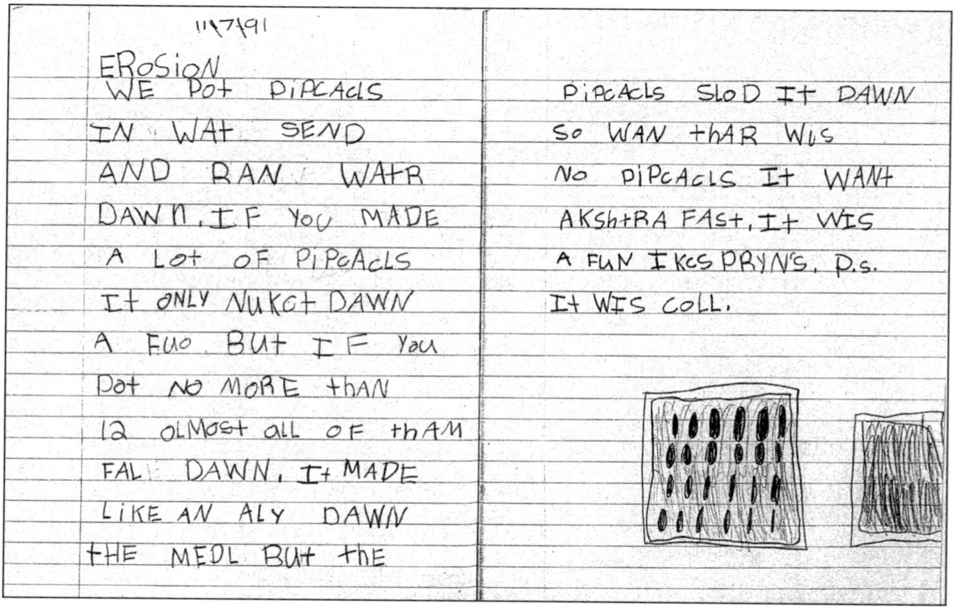

Shannon's report on an experiment on erosion. Her text reads: "We put popsicles [sticks] in wet sand and ran water down. If you made a lot of popsicles, it only knocked down a few. But if you put no more than twelve, almost all of them fall down. It made like an alley down the middle, but the popsicles slowed it down so when there was no popsicles it went extra fast. It was a fun experience. P. S. It was cool."

Figure 9

process it seemed helpful to step back from the work and remind ourselves what needed to be done. One way we did this was to make a list of steps required to complete a game. The list we made on large chart paper looked like this:

1. Research—get information, the facts
2. Make a rough draft
3. Make the game board and cards
4. Write the rules
5. Name your game
6. Test your game

The list became somewhat of a map for all game makers, enabling them to move ahead more clearly focused. Very quickly, abstract ideas took on a concrete form. For example, Kristin, who had spent several days on the draft of her game (shown in Figure 10), was able to write out detailed instructions for players when they landed on specific spaces. Other children, still sorting out concepts they wanted to include in their games, used writing to clarify ideas. When Michele struggled with issues related to air pollution, I suggested that she make a list of things we do to the air—including both those that are good and bad. Once her list was completed, she knew what ideas she needed to include in her game. Margaret, on the other hand, had already completed most steps in the game-making process and only had to add the finishing touches on her game's rules as shown in Figure 11.

The artwork involved in the games was no less exciting. Deanna spent hours of her weekend time coloring nearly one hundred individual squares on her game board about the rain forest, making it a piece of art in its own right. Michael applied his artistic talents to his game about elephants. He approached me one afternoon with the detailed drawing of a leopard shown in Figure 12. He explained that leopards are a danger to elephants. He went on to explain that the small objects he drew near the leopard were going to be game pieces. They were carved elephant tusks obtained by another one of the elephant's enemies: humans.

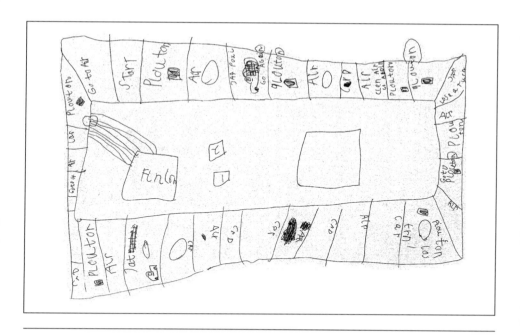

Kristin's air pollution board game.   Figure 10

Rules

① Do Not Takit a wa
② Dont cang your mind
③ Pick a capD
④ Do Not TUOCh
⑤ DONtgoBack Wrds.
⑥ get your Otter To The FINSih Lan.

Margaret's rules for playing her otter board game.   Figure 11

The thinking and time put into the games produced marvelous results. When the artwork was finished and rules were written, it was time to put these games to the test. First with each other, and then with peers and families, we discovered what the roll of the dice would bring.

On our first game-testing day, Michele and I sat at a table playing her game about air pollution. She put down two identical pieces of red macaroni for markers, one for each of us. I asked, "How will we be able to tell them apart?" She paused to study the situation and then went over to the macaroni tub, returned, and replaced one of the red pieces with a green one. We started playing the game again, and she rolled the dice. She landed on a space that said, "Push the button" and got up again. She returned from the math shelf with a button to glue on the board. She said, "It's the smog button." The game continued with each of us moving our marker

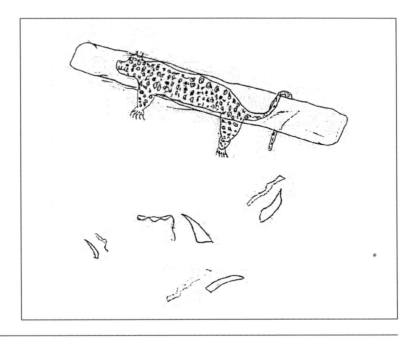

Figure 1 2   Michael's drawing of a leopard.

around her brightly colored game board. Michele came to a space that said, "Go to 71." There was no 71 on her board. She thought about it a minute, and then added a one after a seven on a space. With a few more minor adjustments, we finished playing her game.

Like Michele, many of the children completed their games and were able to play them with each other. Although the games could be played, there were a few details to be worked out. For example, Deanna's rain forest game had a space that said, "Go to the moth," but there was no moth space. Shannon had a similar problem as Michele in that she had made both her game pieces the same color. Also, the blue marker she used had a tendency to rub off on the players. (I became suspicious when I noticed that all players of Shannon's game had blue hands and mouths.) Many of the children used question and answer cards to incorporate the information about their game's topic. Kristin said that Liz's game, "Dolphin Express," was hard to play because she couldn't read Liz's handwriting. She did admit, however, that the game had great information.

Aside from the minor problems, the games had many excellent qualities. The creativity that went into them really showed. In his game, "Rock Rally," Nicholas used different kind of rocks for the markers. Shannon included an interesting twist in her game about water conservation. After she and Nicholas played her game, she told me, "He won my game. It was neat the way he won. I got to the finish first, exactly on the space, but I had five gallons of water, and he didn't waste any water, so he won!"

Jeff and Richard's game, "Tree Rally," had a unique feature: it had different types of money cards to be used to purchase rain forest land. Some cards had dollars and cents, while others had VISA on them. If a player drew the VISA card, he or she could purchase the entire rain forest. Bryce and Jacob incorporated tiny orange krill, the food of many species of whales, into their game, "Underwater Adventure." They had question cards a player could answer to earn more krill, and a trick space that said, "You get all your opponent's krill." They also had a

bonus question: "What do whales eat? (answer): KRILL." A player who answered that one right got to move three extra spaces.
Their game was well designed and easy to play. Libby included
a feature in her game that made it more challenging for people
to win. She placed most of the "Go back to the start" spaces
near the end of the board, toward the finish line.

As I observed the children playing their games, I noticed
two issues related to rules. One had to do with tolerating
ambiguity, and the other involved establishing a firm sense of
right and wrong. For example, while watching Margaret and
Michele play Margaret's otter game, I observed how Margaret
moved her marker. She moved it one space at a time unless
Michele's marker was on the space, and then she would skip
that space. Margaret was perfectly happy to do it this way
until Michele called her on it. Some children allowed these
little idiosyncrasies to happen and others didn't. One day
when Bryce, Brandon, and Jason were playing Bryce's game,
there was a big conflict. Apparently there was a discrepancy
about whether or not a player could count the space he was
occupying as number one, or if the next space should be
number one. In this case it made a big impact on the game's
outcome—if the game were played one way, Jason would get
everyone else's krill; if played the other way, he wouldn't. It
was a good opportunity to talk about rules and to make sure
that everyone knew them at the start of each game. Everyone
agreed that it was okay to change the rules, just as they had
improvised their games all along, but everyone needed to
know the rules for a game in progress. Furthermore, the rules
couldn't be changed unless everyone knew about the change
and agreed to it.

When the games passed the test within our own class,
we asked two groups of people to critique them: the third
and fourth graders next door, and parents. Generally, the
games were well received and there was an appreciation for
all the work that had gone into them. The parents, especially,
were impressed to think that seven- and eight-year-olds could
successfully complete such a project. Along with praise for a
job well done, our game critics offered constructive feedback

for future game making. Most of the problems with the games seemed to focus on unclear rules and directions, not enough cards with information on them, and confusion about how to win the game. We talked about this as a group and thought of ways we could improve on them. Aaron decided he'd remedy some of the problems with his game by writing an instructional manual to go with it. Most of the children decided they'd done their best for this time and happily took their games home.

When the games were finished, I realized that the complex process had produced many layers of learning. The children had made something related to their environment over which they had complete control. They had gained practice with design and composing rules. They had faced the difficult task of incorporating information into game form. And they had learned to put themselves into the position of another who is playing the game for the first time. Inspired by all of these things, I decided to compile a list of concepts included in this process of making games:

likenesses/differences
odd/even numbers
number ordering
taking turns
length
problem solving
revision
prediction
negative space
mental arithmetic
spatial relationships
conservation (of water)
sorting and classifying
moral/ecological responsibility
credit vs. cash
multiplication
one-to-one correspondence
punctuation

writing/reading directions
sequencing
following rules
matching numbers
composition/design
place value
counting
light/dark shades
balancing actual game
    boards
probability
quantitative comparisons
money notation
identifying coins
adding
memorization of facts
directionality

As I looked at the list and reflected on the complex work which had evolved during the months of game making, I felt that it was time well spent. It was a reminder to me that wonderful things occur when children are given the time and patient guidance necessary for transforming their ideas into a tangible product.

My childhood experience of creating miniature environments over a long period of time not only set the stage for the kind of activities my students could do, but also gave me a framework for how I might best work as an educator. I have found that children aren't the only ones who need sustained opportunities to explore and revise their work. Each school year is, in many ways, not unlike the imaginary worlds I created as a child. Rather than working with dolls, miniature cars, and blocks of wood, however, I am working with real people. What and how I played as a child helped me to establish a real-life setting where people can carry out their individual and collective work. Each new year is a chance to make a space in which both the children and adults can learn, a space where each day builds on the previous one—full of adventure, uncertainty, and surprise. Like my imaginary play, this space too has taken time to evolve and grow into the environment it is today. Like a piece of art crafted by hand, it has taken time, care, and thoughtfulness to become realized.

Everyday Life as Content

When we were children, my dad would take us for hikes on Sunday afternoons. No doubt he was just giving my mother a break from all of us for a few hours each week. However, I like to think he was also taking us out to explore the world. We'd often go to the river and walk along its muddy banks. We'd trudge across fields that earlier were lush with that year's crops. I can still feel under my feet the crunchy dried grasses we'd trek through on our way to explore some hidden cave. Some days, along the river road, we'd check out the limestone cliffs that held a key to the mysteries of ancient times—fossils. These outings always seemed like such adventures to me. It was my first exposure to the possibilities of the world outside of my immediate home and school environments.

My inner life as a child was more than full. The environment in which I grew up provided the materials and stimulus for just about anything a child could imagine. For the most part, I lived in a self-contained world, yet it was always good to get out to see new things and visit new places. What I found was that the new experiences enriched my play and added new dimensions to it. As a teacher I have tried to keep this thought in mind. I have not only taken my students out into the world as much as possible, but I've tried to bring in people and current events that would broaden my students' learning experience. It is always fascinating to see how such experiences are incorporated into my students' lives. When we learned that Dr. Seuss had died, we realized what an impact he'd had on our lives, especially when I noticed that *The Cat in the Hat* was written when I was my students' age. The children wanted to put together a collection of Seuss books and do a study of his works. Several children volunteered to bring copies of Seuss books from home.

Bryce and his mother entered the room early the next morning. He told me they had gone to Changing Hands Bookstore the night before and purchased *The Lorax*. He said, "*The Lorax* is in honor of Dr. Seuss and also in honor of the environment." Later our whole class talked about Dr. Seuss, and Richard said, "He wrote all those books and never had a kid!" We read *The Lorax* in class and had a wonderful discussion. The part of the book where the Lorax leaves the stones with the word *UNLESS* provoked dialogue. Jeff said the word has to do with the North Pole getting warm and melting, and the water flooding the Earth. Bryce and Aaron said that it means unless we plant trees, the Earth wouldn't last. Jason said, "He needs to try to figure it out—the Once-ler needs to stop." Then we discussed why the Once-ler is given that name. Bryce said, "He's careless." Aaron added, "He does something once, then he does it again." Robert challenged him, saying, "If he did something once, then did it again, he was doing it more than once! He was only thinking of himself, using resources *once*."

Moved by Dr. Seuss's death, Bryce decided to write a tribute to Dr. Seuss. One day he sat in the author chair during a sharing session and told a little story about when he thought he saw Dr. Seuss in old downtown Tempe but it was just someone attending a dress-up party. After he read his manuscript, one of the children said, "You should include that Dr. Seuss didn't have any kids." Bryce responded with, "I bet he knew a lot of them, though." Weeks later, after taking into account his classmates' responses to his manuscript, Bryce again sat in the author chair, this time holding his newly published book, *The Great Dr. Seuss*. The text read as follows:

Dr. Seuss died when he was 87 in 1991. He was a good man. He gave to the poor. He also gave to stop pollution.

When I was little and sick my mom would read one of his stories and I would become cheerful again. When he was little he thought of a lot of funny words and when he was an adult he put them together and he made 48 books.

Once I thought I saw him but it was someone dressed up as him and when my mom told me that it wasn't him I laughed and laughed 'til my face was red. I had to drink a big glass of water a lot of times to cool myself down.

In the best of times he won best author and illustrator. I voted for him in both categories. My favorite book of his is *The Lorax* and my second favorite one is *The Grinch Who Stole Christmas* [*sic*]. I like the part in *The Lorax* when the Lorax said that the Once-ler couldn't sell the Thneed and he did for three ninety-eight.

And now let's hope there will be another Dr. Seuss.

Bryce finished his book by reading the author description of himself. He had written, "He wrote this book because of his interest in writing and because he likes Dr. Seuss."

Like many of his peers, Bryce chose to include important current events as part of his daily learning. What was important to him in the world also became important in school. Making everyday life a part of the school curriculum gives children a chance to process events that have occurred. It gives them time to think and to reflect on happenings that have had a direct or indirect impact on their lives. Through writing his tribute to Dr. Seuss, Bryce was able to honor a writer who enriched his own life as well as the lives of millions of other adults and children. At the same time, writing his book gave Bryce a chance to work through his feelings of loss in a constructive, meaningful way.

When children study and write about issues of the world that are important to them, it also gives them greater opportunities to make connections within their everyday work in the classroom. It broadens their base of knowledge. After we read a chapter of *The Real Thief* by William Steig, one of the children commented that Steig sure uses strange words. We decided to make a list we called "Strange Words from Steig." One of the words was *Kalikak,* from the Kalikak diamond. I couldn't find it in the dictionary, and someone said, "Well, Mary, everything isn't in the dictionary!" I told them I thought it was a made-up word; Steig does that occasionally. Bryce said, "That's just like Dr. Seuss. It's like a Seuss word. He made words up all the time too!" Bryce's passion for Dr. Seuss helped to bridge his own emerging knowledge with that of his peers.

When the richness of life is given a respected place in the daily curriculum, it brings all sorts of surprises. In fact, the surprises are what keep the curriculum interesting and alive. When life itself is counted on to inform the direction of school learning, it fosters a certain wide-awakeness. Teachers and children who practice viewing the world with this attitude come to expect the unexpected as part of their daily routine—and in the process often find themselves in the midst of exciting, unexplored learning opportunities.

One beautiful October morning, we had just finished reading *Diego,* the life story of the painter Diego Rivera. Each of the book's illustrations has colorful borders. Our conversation about the book's artwork inspired someone to ask, "Could we go to sketch the crane today?"

The children were fascinated with the gigantic crane we noticed in our wanderings about the neighborhood. It was located at a nearby dairy plant and was being used on the construction site to add a tower to the plant. The children wanted to see it again. The morning invited outdoor work, so we gathered our clipboards and headed out to see what we could discover.

Our explorations of the neighborhood opened the door to life in our immediate surroundings. Some discoveries, such as the mechanics smoking cigarettes (see chapter six), served as serious reminders about the choices we make that could influence our future. Other things we noticed provided us with opportunities to enjoy a fascinating process—and at the same time sharpen our observational skills. One result of paying closer attention to our neighborhood was that many of the children were becoming quite adept at making detailed drawings, as demonstrated in Deanna's rendition of the dairy plant shown in Figure 13.

Deanna's drawing of a construction site near the school.

Figure 13

The visits to the construction site did more than satisfy our curiosity and develop the children's drawing skills. They served as a means of constructing a new kind of understanding with our science work. At the same time that the crane was busy with the assembly of the tower, the children took on an assignment in class to build a structure that had two requirements:

1. It had to have at least two levels.
2. It had to be designed so that an object (e.g., a marble) could move from one level to another.

Using recycled materials such as paper towel tubes, Styrofoam trays, egg cartons, and cardboard (with lots of tape), the children went to work on their structures. Nicholas discovered a way to make a joint out of a Styrofoam tray so that the marble would make a smooth transition through a bend in the tube.

Later he and Jason added another tube so the marble could roll through a choice of two openings. Robert and Bryce made a long tube that they held up so that the marble shot out the tube, flew through space, and then, when their engineering was most accurate, landed in their structure's other tube and came out the end. Bryce wrote about the problems he encountered as he developed his design, as shown in Figure 14.

The visits to sketch the crane and the work on the marble structures stood on their own as worthwhile activities filled with surprises. But the real surprise came for me on the last day of October when we made another trip to the dairy plant. On this day the crane was lifting a huge U-shaped pipe high in the air and attaching it to a shiny silver dome that only days before had been resting on the ground in front of us.

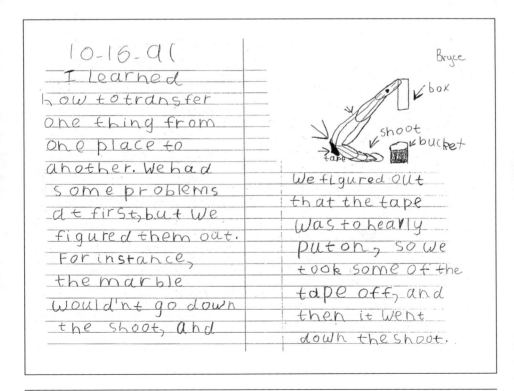

Figure 14   Bryce's report on building a chute for rolling marbles.

A man noticed us and walked over to ask what we were doing. We told him we were sketching, and Robert immediately began firing questions at him. He wanted to know if the smoke coming out of the pipe in the plant was pollution. The man said it was just steam. Shannon and Liz wanted to know how long they had been building the plant and if he was the boss. They had quickly written out questions for this impromptu interview. I asked if they ever gave tours, and he said they didn't because of health department regulations. Robert became excited about all of this and said, "We could make a book about the plant! We'll have to come here often!" When the man said it was going to be a powdered milk plant, Michele said, "I'm going to make some peanut butter play dough. I'm going to wait until they make it [the powdered milk] at this plant, and I'll buy it here." Jeff and Richard, fascinated by the construction workers welding high above the ground, were engrossed in their drawing, shown in Figure 15.

When we returned to school, the children all shared what they had drawn and we talked about the big U-shaped pipe. I could see that Shannon was struggling with a big idea. I asked her to talk about her thinking. She was trying to figure out how the pipe would work. Evidently she and Richard had had a conversation over at the plant about it. They were thinking that if one tried to put a marble in it like in the structures they'd made, the marble wouldn't go back down because it couldn't turn the corner of the pipe. I reminded them that the man said it was going to be a pipe for hot air and the air would be able to travel through it easily. We talked about how the air could move through the U-shaped curve in a different way than a marble could because air isn't solid. I noticed from the look on Shannon's face that she finally understood. As we finished this conversation, I congratulated the children on their excellent thinking and told them once again that it is when we put ideas together like this, connecting different experiences in our lives, that we learn the most. Sometimes they are connections with things we observe and work we do. At other times they are with people—our families in particular.

Figure 15   Jeff and Richard's drawing of the powdered-milk factory construction site.

On the day before Veterans' Day, I read Eve Bunting's *The Wall,* which led to a short discussion about the various wars and what the Wall represents. For the previous night's homework, I had asked the children to find out if anyone in their families was a veteran and to tell a story about that person. I planned for us to make a graph of which war each veteran was in and what each did in the service. The variety was surprising.

The children told stories of everything from a messenger who ended up with shrapnel in his head to an entertainer who sang for the troops. Many stories were about WWII veterans, but there were also quite a few from Vietnam and the Persian Gulf. Deanna reported about her relative who had fought in a war in South America. I was surprised by how many fathers had been in the service. Michael's story was by far the most touching. It was about his father, who had died the previous year. I could see that Michael had spent a long time the night before, meticulously writing out his story in cursive; eventually, he typed it on the computer. He dedicated his tribute to the police department where his father had worked (Figure 16).

```
The wall has lots of people names.
Some of these people was friend
of my dad.Myd dad was in vite nam
for one year .He didnt get shot.
He put bullets on hes chrictmas
tree.He jumped out of airplanes.
it was scary in the war. he
carried two guns.My dad/s nickname
was sugar bear.He had a rafel gun
He was in swat .He was in the war
and the arme and a police man.

          by dad

          by michael.
          and mom
          and justin.

          to the police
building
```

Michael's tribute to his father.

Figure 16

Inquiring about family history helped the children know and remember the people who came before them who had shaped their own lives in certain ways. It enabled them to see where their families fit into historical events. Researching family information also opened up new channels of communication. Nicholas's mom reported how pleased she was with the assignment. She said that Nicholas voluntarily called both grandmothers to find out the information he needed.

The bonds established with each other and with the people we encountered—younger children in the school, members of our families—gave us a chance to find our place in the world. We felt more connected to the range of human feelings and possibilities. When we heard Michael's story of his brave father, we felt proud for him and at the same time sad, knowing that his memories of his dad are all he will carry with him as he grows up.

On the other hand, stories of accomplishment gave us an opportunity to celebrate. One day Deanna entered the room all excited and announced that her grandmother from Colombia would become a U. S. citizen that day. Because we all knew her grandmother, we decided to honor this significant event in Berta's life by making her a gigantic red, white, and blue card and having the other children in the school sign it. We wanted to do this for Berta because she was always so loving and cheerful to all of us. It made us feel good about ourselves when we knew that we could help someone else celebrate the fulfillment of a dream.

Each time we heard a new family story, it opened an additional window for understanding the child who told the story. It also gave us new insight into understanding ourselves. Katherine Paterson (1990) writes, "We are trying to communicate that which lies in our deepest heart, which has no words, which can only be hinted at through the means of a story." Sharing family histories enabled us to appreciate each child's uniqueness, to get at what can't be said with words and at the same time see how we experience similar human feelings. On the day before Thanksgiving, we talked about the children's family Thanksgiving traditions. Jacob said one of his traditions is that his mom always eats her pumpkin pie first so she won't be too stuffed for it. Nicole told of how her family always invites someone over from the university whose family lives far away. Shannon said her grandma always takes so long to make the food that everyone tries to get there late. After they eat they play a lot of sports outside. Jason said they celebrate differently each year, and this year he was planning to put a whoopie cushion where his dad would sit. Richard said they'd be at his grandma's in Tucson and that they usually rent tables. When I heard their stories, I recalled my own, especially those from my childhood. I was reminded quickly of the value of teachers sharing their family stories too. I realized that the stories of my everyday life as a child needed to be a part of theirs. This insight was strongly confirmed for me when we were working on our annual holiday poetry collection.

Every year, we make a collection of holiday poems to give to the children's families. Soon after we had begun working on this project, I had to go to Seattle to attend a conference. When I returned just before Thanksgiving, I was excited to tell the class about my trip. I told them of seeing Mount Saint Helens from the airplane and about feeding french fries to the seagulls down at Ivar's near the shore. I talked about going to the Space Needle and about the ferry ride over to Bainbridge Island. I told them of spending time with my friend Georgia Heard, the poet, and I showed them the book I had gotten autographed by Barbara Cooney. They enjoyed hearing my stories, and we all felt glad to be back together.

When it was time for writing, I asked how they were doing on their poetry for our holiday collection. They said fine. When I walked around the room to check in with individuals, I was disappointed to see that many of them had regressed to poems like this:

Thanksgiving is fun
Thanksgiving is turkey and gravy
Thanksgiving is a family time
Thanksgiving . . . Thanksgiving . . . Thanksgiving

Their writing was very general, with little personal commitment. I could see that we had our work cut out for us. When I saw what happened with their poetry during the three days I was away, I realized that I needed to bring stories from the outside to enrich their lives, especially as writers. I had to help them see other possibilities by exposing them to experiences beyond their own.

We talked about the difference between a poem that is general and one that gives small details that let the reader inside the writer's world. It seemed that the only way I could get this point across was through a personal example. I decided to share the first few lines of a poem I was writing about my childhood Thanksgivings:

> Perhaps it's the absence of all the cousins
> that leaves me feeling empty this time of year
>
> So far away from the dreary Midwestern mornings
> when my parents would awaken us early
> > tumbling our sleepy bodies out of bed
> > into the family car
>
> For the drive past frozen towns and cornfields
> to the massive brick house where my great-aunt lived

When I read these lines, it opened up a dialogue about details. Many of the children began to see that through the details—the small, ordinary things that are often taken for granted—real stories are told. When I talked to them about the details I remember of my childhood Thanksgivings—playing football on the lawn with all my cousins, the frozen cornfields, my great-aunt's big brick house—they began to see how they could include similar details in their writing. I was hoping it was an understanding that would stay with them as they progressed as writers during the rest of the year. And I hoped they would come to realize that when we take the time to share the rich details of our lives with others, we too are enriched.

As our awareness of human possibilities broadened through sharing family stories, life gained passage into the curriculum through other avenues as well. We learned more about certain aspects of life (or was that lice?) than we ever cared to know.

One morning a small group of girls was gathered in a corner of the classroom for their literature study. Laura, our student teacher, was leading the group as her supervisor from the university sat nearby to observe her emerging teaching skills. One of the girls got up from the discussion and approached me saying, "Mary, my head itches." Her friend, also in the group, added, "Mine does too." I feared the worst. Having dealt with this problem before, I took them outside and checked their hair. Sure enough, they both had head lice. After calling their exasperated parents to come pick them up, I checked the rest of the class. Another girl had them, too. The literature group dwindled to two children, and the university supervisor decided to make a quick exit. I looked at the three girls as they waited to be taken home to be rid of the hidden cargo in their hair, and all I could do was laugh. Just when I thought I had everything under control, I was reminded that the only predictable aspect of teaching is the element of surprise.

During the next two weeks, I fumigated the room twice, removed the pillows and dress-ups, discovered another case of lice, and spent an inordinate amount of time sitting with the four girls, checking their hair—and chatting. Although it was a stressful situation we all wanted to be over, especially when I had to send one of them home with a newly discovered crop of nits, it did produce some positive results. It gave us time to slow things down a bit and just be together. As I watched these girls deal with being sent home, fielding questions from their curious peers ("Do you *still* have *lice?*"), and sitting patiently while adults carefully removed the nits from their hair, I developed a new appreciation for the girls. They were good sports, and they faced the challenge of this menacing problem with the same strength they had demonstrated when they faced each other in past situations, particularly in conflicts on the playground. In addition to my renewed appreciation for these girls, the lice experience had another positive side benefit. It eliminated their fighting on the playground, for a while anyway. Certainly it was a matter of timing and circumstances, but it was a huge relief to everyone involved—particularly me.

Long after the lice fiasco was over, two of the girls decided to take it one step further by writing a book of lice jokes as a surprise for their parents. Figure 17 shows one of their jokes. They ended their book with this description of themselves as authors:

Figure 17   A joke about lice. The text reads: "Q: Why does lice have claws? A: 'Cuz it's in the family of dogs."

They both like pets. They both had lice and hated it. They loved working together on this book. They decided to write this book because their publisher encouraged them to do it. They both agree that Mary was a wonderful teacher. Their final statement about lice is: WE HATE LICE!!!

The lice experience, aside from the stressful aspect of it, carried many surprises. Along with the slowing down and the girls' new appreciation for each other, it provided an opportunity to take an apparently negative experience and find humor in it. It became a chance to create a piece of writing to entertain those who previously had been made to suffer through the ordeal of getting rid of the annoying creatures. On a deeper level, it was a lesson for all of us that life will occasionally present experiences that we view as trouble, and it's our job to see that we handle them in the best way possible. Even though a situation can cause us to feel annoyed or frustrated, there is always a side of any experience from which we can grow—and even laugh. When we allow life to be part of our daily curriculum, whether it comes from family stories, visiting lice, or everyday events, we all have the opportunity to become more aware as human beings. When we are more aware, we are able to respond more fully and more compassionately.

CHAPTER EIGHT

A Vision of Inclusion

I was deeply attached to my dolls when I was a girl. I had all kinds of dolls—baby dolls, a life-sized doll, Barbies, my trolls (of course), exotic dolls my grandmothers brought me from other countries, and the small, cheap plastic ones from the dime store. I felt such loyalty to each of them. I can remember lying in my bed on Christmas Eve with my favorites lined up beside me. I was excited in anticipation of the new doll I hoped to receive the next morning. Yet sometimes I felt sad and cried for the old ones. I would talk to my dolls and reassure them that even though I was getting a new one, each would still be loved. I wanted all of my dolls to know I would always have a place for them in my heart. I didn't want anyone to feel left out.

It's hard to know where the seeds of compassion are first germinated. Certainly the example of our parents, teachers, and peers influences how we learn to interact with people around us. For some of us, the potential for compassion and tolerance seems to be innately stronger. For others, it takes a bit more nurturing to cultivate such qualities. I'm not sure where it began for me. I do know that for as long as I can remember, being included has been an issue.

I always felt different as a child. In retrospect it seems that I spent a good bit of time alone, thinking about the world and my place in it. I knew I wanted to do something different from anything I'd seen around me, but I wasn't sure what that would be. Even at a young age, I felt a sensitivity toward those who suffered in the world. Although our community didn't have the problems normally associated with larger cities, (e.g., racial disagreements, homelessness, crime), I was keenly aware that others existed who didn't have everything I had. I had deeply burning questions about life, but there was no one at that point who could answer them, so I tended to feel isolated. Certainly I had friends to play with, especially in the neighborhood. But in school, it seemed like so much energy was devoted to gaining the acceptance of my peers. I always struggled to feel included, to feel as if I belonged. That struggle, as much as anything, has made me aware not only of dynamics of acceptance within the immediate class-room environment, but of the need to include content work in the curriculum which deals with it as well.

Each year my class embarks on a study of human rights. It is a study I select, yet the children have a strong say in the direction the study will take. The focus almost always emerges from the children's comments, questions, and inter-ests. In past years we have studied Africa, Native Americans, the Underground Railroad and Harriet Tubman, the Civil Rights Movement, and the lives of individuals such as Mahatma Gandhi, Martin Luther King Jr., Rosa Parks, Frederick Douglass, and George Washington Carver. The emphasis is on learning to understand how people are differ-ent yet similar, and how to prevent the problems of the past from recurring. We talk about what we can do on a daily basis to avoid these patterns. For example, we work on treat-ing each other compassionately by putting ourselves in some-one else's position. We ask ourselves how we would feel if we were being mistreated. I often begin to see glimmers of interest in this study long before it takes place.

One morning Bryce entered the classroom wearing a pin of Martin Luther King Jr. on his denim jacket. His mom had bought it for him. He said, "I thought it'd go into our long talks about being kind." King became the subject of fur-ther conversation after we read *Diego,* a book about the painter Diego Rivera that includes paintings of people being shot by soldiers. One of the children asked why the artist

chose to paint people getting killed. This set off a whole discussion of MLK and why he was shot. During a poetry study,
we read Nikki Giovanni's poem "ten years old" and talked
about the word *race* in it. We talked about the various mean-
ings of *race*, and our conversation inevitably led to a discussion of civil rights. Aaron was excited about the content of
our talk, and I could tell he had a big idea in his mind as he
left the room to wash his hands for lunch. Upon returning in
a hyperventilated state, he said, "Mary, sometimes I just *respi-
rate* hearing what I know about Martin Luther King!"

The struggle for human rights had surfaced in other
ways prior to our official classroom study. One significant
event was our schoolwide production of John Cech's book
My Grandmother's Journey. Traditionally our school has celebrated the Winter Solstice each year by giving a program for
parents and families. The evening always includes singing,
dance, drama, and lively costumes. As a staff we have experimented with different approaches to the event, and this year
was no exception. We decided to try an all-school production, with multi-aged groups (four-year-olds through
ten-year-olds) presenting each section. Our plan was to do an
interpretation of *My Grandmother's Journey*, the story of a
woman and her family's escape to freedom during war times.
Teachers teamed up to collaborate on each section.

After reading the book and talking about it several
times, we began meeting in groups. My group's assignment
was to depict the darkness of the war through dance. We
called our piece "The Dance of Darkness." For three weeks
we worked on it, an hour and a half each morning. The
rehearsals were not without their frustrations, especially trying to contain the energy of four-year-olds while giving older
children the opportunity to create their own choreography.
Frequently we wondered if we'd made the right decision by
organizing the children the way we had. But everyone perse-
vered, and on the night of the performance it all paid off.

Parents eagerly await each year's Winter Solstice
Celebration, wondering if it will match what they've seen in the
past. As this evening unfolded, they were not disappointed.

Children in festive costumes sat with their teachers in a large circle on the wooden floor. One group at a time, the children took their places to perform. The children playing the lead characters showed the struggle of the family as they found their way to freedom. Large group dances filled in various parts of the story. Then it was time for "The Dance of Darkness." Boys and girls of all sizes, wearing dark clothing and elaborate masks they had made, prepared for their dance. The older children helped younger ones get ready for their entrance.

The dance began with four dancers—three representing the light and one, the darkness. The single dancer of darkness stayed in the background like a shadow. The light struggled to remain free as more dancers of darkness entered the stage. Each time they were confined, they found a way to escape. When the music changed to a more forceful rhythmic pattern, ranks of dancers depicting soldiers marched in from either side. It was strong and powerful movement. Then they unfurled three large pieces of black cloth, one for each group on stage. The cloths were lifted, turned, and waved by the children surrounding each piece of fabric. In the final moments of the dance, the children formed long passageways with the cloths as the tops. The dance concluded with each of the dancers of light emerging triumphantly in the front of a group. It was poetry through movement.

After each group contributed its part to the story, the program ended. There were few dry eyes in the audience as proud families clapped and cheered. Everyone was moved by the proficiency with which the children delivered their lines, sang their songs, and performed their dances. But more than that, they were touched by the amount of care the children demonstrated toward each other. They recognized the powerful connection made between children of all ages who accomplished what they had because of relationships built on trust and respect. They also appreciated the level of caring among the teachers, acknowledging that through the teachers' example, the children had established that trust. Ten-year-old Charlie, whose family fled from Latvia in similar fashion many years ago, wrote about the experience the next day:

> I thought the Solstice was very moving to me. It reminded me of
> my own grandmother and how my family had to get any jobs
> they could. I was also crying at the event . . . I was crying of hap-
> piness and I thought it was very different from most of the years.
> But I think it worked very well and I was really glad to be a part
> of the Solstice and glad to be a part of Awakening Seed.

The images and memories of that evening made a strong
impression on each of us. Like Charlie, we were all glad to
be a part of such a powerful event. It set the tone for further
studies of human rights and became a reference point of
images that would seep into our hearts and minds in subtle,
yet profound, ways. This awareness surfaced in the literature
we read together, in discussions that followed, and in the various projects that emerged as a result.

Weeks after our Winter Solstice Celebration, we began
our focused study of human rights. I have found that literature
is the best way to enter into a study of this nature, and I generally rely on good books to get us started. One day I was
reading *Nettie's Trip South* by Ann Turner. We instantly
became involved in a discussion of a line about a slave auctioneer who wears a "tight white suit." A few of the children
had just finished a small-group literature study of the book
and wanted to speak first. Aaron said that the tight white suit
represents the auctioneer's tightness against black people.
Brandon said, "The suit is protecting blacks from coming in
and coming after the whites." I tried to help them see that the
suit can also be seen as an armor, as in the medieval ages.
Jason said, "The suit is like an armor to keep his [the auctioneer's] power in—it is like a symbol to keep his power in. He
is hiding his evilness." Then someone mentioned that maybe
the man is showing his evilness and trying to hide his friend-
liness. Aaron finally declared, "Dr. King wanted whites and
blacks to use very little evilness and more kindness."

Shortly after our discussion of *Nettie's Trip South*, we
undertook Virginia Hamilton's collection of African American
folk tales, *The People Could Fly*. In the first story about jungle
animals, the class laughed hysterically at the silly lion's line:

"Me and myself, me and myself." Every time it was repeated throughout the story, the laughter became louder. When we finished reading for the day, we talked about the story. Right away Jeff commented that there is a lesson in it: The lion shouldn't scare other animals. This led to a conversation about bullying others and how it isn't right.

We appreciated the book's humor on the next day as well. When we came to the line "The cock crowed," I asked if anyone knew what that meant. There was no reply, so I explained that a cock is a rooster. As we read on, we came to a part in another story where a turtle was being carried under an eagle's wing and was complaining about the foul odor. I said, "Maybe it was its wingpit!" Richard said, "No, it was his cockpit!" Then Robert added that the eagle needed "birdeodorant." By then the hilarity had reached a peak. After the silliness settled, Aaron said, "The legends in Africa were meant to be true." Jeff came up with another idea about the story's lesson when he commented, "This story is to teach people to not be greedy."

Although humor was a predominant characteristic of the stories, we began to see patterns that were more serious. After hearing two or three stories, the children noticed that each one has a lesson or moral. They also noticed that many of the same animal characters are in each folk tale and have specific characteristics. For example, the rabbit is always smart and likes to play tricks. Another similarity the children noticed in all the stories is the dialect. Although the folk tales originated from all over the world, there is a specific dialect present, as seen in the phrase that begins each story, "Once a time." Our discussion of dialect led into one about slavery. One of the children said that the stories make you want to know more about slaves and why they told stories so much. During one conversation Nicole said, "The slaves are telling you how they feel." In other words, without saying it directly, they are expressing the fact that they don't like to be told what to do by someone else. They say it instead through story.

Our conversations about slavery, originating from humorous African American folk tales, led us to serious questions. How could some human beings treat others so unfairly?

Why has it taken so long for changes to be made? Why are some people so afraid to give up power? It was a perfect lead-in to our study of the Civil Rights Movement and individuals throughout history who have promoted human rights. Little did we know that one of the most important figures of the Civil Rights Movement would come so close to touching our classroom circle.

One morning Aaron burst through the door and announced to the class that he and his mom had been invited to ride on the bus to meet Rosa Parks at the airport the following Thursday night. Shannon asked, "Who is Rosa Parks?" Jeff, who had seen me sorting out the monthly issues of *Scholastic News*, replied immediately, "She's the girl in *Scholastic News*." I explained that she is the woman who, in 1955, started the Montgomery, Alabama, bus boycott by refusing to give up her seat to a white person. It seemed like an opportune moment to present the feature article in that week's issue of *Scholastic News*.

After reading the article in pairs, we decided to act out the bus scene. Even though Martin Luther King Jr. was not a designated character in the immediate scene, Aaron insisted on being MLK since he, like King, is African American. We acted out the story of Rosa Parks, including her being hauled off to jail for refusing to cooperate with the authorities. At the end Aaron gave a wonderful impromptu performance as MLK, using a bellowing voice to give his speech. When it was over, Michele said she had a comment. She wondered, "Next time could you use a softer voice?" I mentioned that MLK spoke with a forceful voice, and Richard, grasping for an appropriate measurement word, said, "Yeah, MLK spoke 1,000 mg loud!"

If there was one word that described our class study of human rights, it was passion. Aaron was contagiously passionate, and others quickly took on the topic with great enthusiasm. After our reenactment of the Rosa Parks story, Jason wrote in his daily writing book the entry shown in Figure 18. Bryce soon followed with his poem about racial issues, shown in Figure 19. Discussions about the Ku Klux

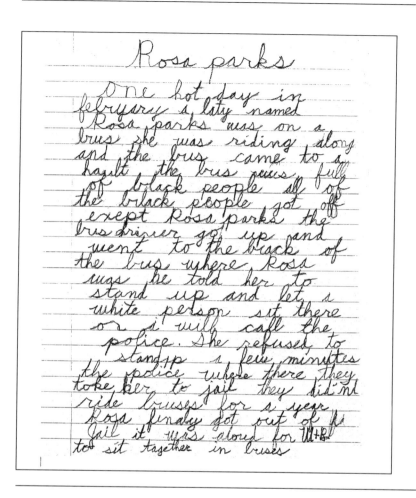

Rosa parks

One hot day in february a laty named Rosa parks was on a bus she was riding along and the bus came to a haylt the bus was full of black people all of the black people got off exept Rosa parks the bus driver got up and went to the black of the bus where Rosa was he told her to stand up and let a white person sit there or i will call the police. She refused to stand up a few minutes the police where there they toke her to jail they did'nt ride bruses for a year Rosa finaly got out of jail it was aloud for MLK to sit together in buses

Jason's essay on Rosa Parks.

Figure 18

Klan caused nearly everyone to become excited, especially when Aaron stood up and dramatically demonstrated how large some of the burning crosses were.

One day as we were reading about the marches and boycotts, one of the children thought it was just black people being jailed and shot with the high pressure fire hose. I told them that some white people were also involved because they wanted the laws changed, too. I told them of a movie I

```
Whites Hated Blacks

          by Bryce Gerrich

Whites had no good judgement
they treated blacks
like ants
they said they were all dirty
and had them as
their slaves
they whipped them
'til they nearly died
they died and so
 did

Martin Luther King, J.R.
```

Figure 19   Bryce's poem, "Whites Hated Blacks."

had recently seen about a white woman who supported the
bus boycott by helping with car pooling. This led to a discussion of why white women were generally more supportive
than white men of the work of King, particularly in the South.
We talked about how white women have also been sup-
pressed by the men in control. The issue of fear came up; that
is, if a person has been cruel to others, he or she wouldn't
want to make those others more powerful because they'd
seek revenge. This set off further discussion about white male
supremacy. The interest was overwhelming.

   To keep track of our study, we made a time line of individuals who have shaped the Civil Rights Movement. In addition to Rosa Parks and MLK, we included Frederick Douglass,
the great abolitionist; Gandhi; Harriet Tubman; and John F.
Kennedy. One of the most interesting things we noticed was
how lives overlap. We spent a good bit of time adding and sub-
tracting ages, finding out how old someone was when he or

she died, and for how many years certain individuals, such as Gandhi and MLK, were alive at the same time. It was fascinating to see how lives connect with each other. It was also fascinating when the children made connections to their own lives. One day, after we had read about the heavy weight a slave owner threw at Harriet Tubman's forehead, someone's lunch box fell and bumped Deanna on the head. Libby tried to cheer her up by saying, "Oh well, you can be like Harriet Tubman!"

A key factor in the success of our civil rights study was direct contact with people who were actively involved in the movement. Aaron was fortunate to be able to see Rosa Parks in person and, although he didn't get to ask her the questions he had planned to, he caught a glimpse of her and briefly spoke to her. When he brought his experience of seeing this strong, gentle woman back to the class, we were all impressed. Another person who brought her experiences to our class was Elsie, Aaron's mother.

On the same day Aaron saw Rosa Parks, his mother came to school to talk about her life growing up in Virginia. We had heard her poignant stories about racial discrimination in past years, and had invited her back to tell us more. Elsie talked about her early years, about not understanding the adults' violent reaction one day when she held hands in a country store with another little four-year-old, a white child. She told us of her painful and lonely high school years when she was the first black student to integrate an all-white high school. We heard of her friend who would only speak to her when no one else was around. When Elsie told us all the mean and cruel names the other students called her, Deanna asked, "Did your almost friend say things too?"

Elsie's stories had a profound impact on each of us who heard them. We decided to write letters to thank her for coming to speak with us. Bryce ended his letter by saying, "I think you're the next Martin Luther King Jr!!" Robert wrote, "I do not think it was fair that they judged you by the color of your skin and not your personality."

Elsie's stories, and those that arose from our civil rights study, will remain with us—for they are stories that have brought us to a closer understanding of how we connect to people of all races throughout history. They are stories that remind us of what we need to do to see that the rights of all people are protected. Her stories gave us insight into the hardship and commitment of the people who have stepped to the forefront in the struggle for equal human rights.

As our study progressed, the focus shifted to Abraham Lincoln and the Civil War. The children were fascinated with Lincoln's life, especially the stories of his childhood. They were impressed that he grew to be 6′4″ tall. In a humorous moment Aaron said, "I bet if Lincoln was alive we'd all look up to him!" Brandon picked up on Aaron's pun and said, "Yeah. We'd really admire him, too."

One of the children asked when Lincoln died. Aaron thought he remembered reading it in a book about U.S. presidents, so he got up to find the book. While he was looking, I read them a 1939 book about Lincoln that won the Caldecott Award (*Abraham Lincoln* by Ingri d'Aulaire and Edgar Parin d'Aulaire). Someone asked how many years ago 1939 was, and it turned into a math problem: $1992 - 1939 =$ _____. Aaron returned with the book on presidents and told us Lincoln died in 1865. Another math problem arose: How old would Lincoln be today if he were still alive? The curiosity about lives and numbers seemed to be a never-ending quality of this group.

As our civil rights study begins to wind down, we believe it is important to celebrate our knowledge. Each year the focus of the study varies, and our way of celebrating changes from year to year as well. Some years we write a collection of poetry. To do this we make a list of topics we have covered and each child chooses which one is of most interest to him or her. When they start on their poems, I encourage them to say what they want to say in a new way. They help each other as they share what they have written. When Laura shared her poem about Gandhi, she read the ending, "And now I know a boy named Aaron," meaning that because of Gandhi's efforts, it is possible for black and white children to be friends. While Aaron appreciated her thought, he requested that she say *person* instead of *boy* because *boy* has carried such a negative connotation in African American history.

Such attention to detail on lines produced excellent results. One child's ideas fed off of another's as they included imagery and metaphor that came right from the heart of our study. When Liz shared her poem about the Ku Klux Klan, she read the line "their hearts were ten sizes too small." She offered everyone a suggestion for finding poem ideas when she told us she got the idea from *How the Grinch Stole Christmas*. Richard gave us a powerful new metaphor when he wrote about the moss that Harriet Tubman used to find her way north. His completed poem is shown in Figure 20. Everyone agreed that his line "the moss was like a compass to freedom" was classroom poetry at its finest.

The Compass to Freedom

Moss helped
Harriet Tubman
on cold rainy nights
all she had to do
was feel
on the north side of a tree
and that is the way
they should go

and she did
and she helped
over 300 slaves
escape
the moss
was like a compass
to freedom

by Richard Hobson

Richard's poem, "The Compass to Freedom."

Figure 20

Other children produced poems that were sensitive and
profound. Jacob captured the essence of Gandhi's frustrations
with a line describing "their hard and sad problems." Jason
wrote his poem as a rap, illustrated in Figure 21. And Liz
made a commitment to both the past and the future with her
poem "Dream Maker," shown in Figure 22.

When everyone's poem was finished, the children each
made a collage illustration of it for a class book and a black
line illustration for the collection to be duplicated and sent
home. Their illustrations were no less wonderful than their
poetry. Steffen meticulously placed small white rectangles on
a black strip of road—the road John F. Kennedy traveled past

could have been better

martin luther king
won
the nobel peace prize
all of a sudden
he got shot
in the head
and then in a snap
he
just drops dead

i think the guy
that shot him
should have gotten a letter
that his life
could
have been a lot
better
if he hadn't shot
m.l.k.

by Jason

Figure 21   Jason's poem, "could have been better."

Dream Maker

Martin Luther King, Jr.
I'll keep your dream alive
my black friends
are waiting
for me

I get black friends
from you
Martin Luther King, Jr.

you're my dream maker

by Elizabeth Ziegler

Elizabeth's poem, "Dream Maker."   Figure 22

the book depository on his fateful day in Dallas in 1963. Deanna cut out tiny hands and feet for her illustration of MLK's famous "I Have A Dream" speech. Their illustrations were as lively as the artists who created them.

Other years we have made quilts. Each child took weeks to sew a quilt block, which was then pieced together with blocks made by the rest of the class. One year, to celebrate this piece of art, we decided to have a tea for the parents and invite them to come see the quilt and hear the songs and words that had taken on new meaning for us during our study. It was a memorable event.

The children took their places excitedly on the floor, facing the guests we had invited for the big event. After a brief period of rustling papers and negotiating the seating arrangement, eight-year-old Danielle stood and welcomed our guests:

Thank you for coming to THE FREEDOM THAT'S ALWAYS BEEN
WANTED QUILT TEA. One of the reasons we did the quilt is
because there are lots of quilts in the stories we read. For example, Harriet Tubman had a quilt. She took it with her when she
took her people to freedom. When she came to the first Quaker
house, she met a nice lady there. When Harriet left she gave the
Quaker lady her quilt for helping her. The quilt was her only pos-
session. Slaves had quilts instead of blankets because they did not
have enough fabric of one kind, so they just used the scraps.
They had to make quilts. Our first encounter with quilts was
when we were invited to the ASU museum. They had lots of different quilts on display. When we made our quilt we each drew
the part of the study we wanted to do for the quilt. Then we each
picked the background for our quilt block. We gathered our fabric and we cut out the shapes we wanted. Then we sewed them
onto the quilt block. When everyone was done with their blocks,
Mary sewed it together and quilted it. We each drew a picture
and wrote a poem or speech about our quilt block.

When Danielle finished reading, Kevin stood with the pointer in
his hand by the recently finished quilt hanging on the chalkboard
behind the half-circle of children. One by one, each child stood
and read the poem or description of the quilt block he or she had
contributed to the finished piece. As each child spoke, Kevin
pointed to the appropriate block. When it was his turn, Kevin read
his moving poem about Harriet Tubman and the slave auction:

A Very Brave Slave

Harriet Tubman
once was a slave
She was a very brave slave
When she was little
her brothers were getting sold

Yes sold

Sold in a slave auction
I bet she hated the auction for that
I bet you would

I know
I would

When all of the quilt blocks had been described, the presentation concluded with our favorite civil rights song, "We Shall Overcome." Kjirsten, a gentle and timid girl, stood bravely to sing a solo verse. Not a single heart remained unmoved by the purity of her voice. It was a perfect tribute to our study focused on the dreams of freedom and human rights—pieced together by people of various heritages and cultures.

Bringing the study to a close by celebrating knowledge—through art and poetry, or by making a quilt—is as important to the learning process as each step that has come before. Through the act of celebrating, "we recognize that people have the power to incorporate the joys and achievements of other people into their lives" (Peterson 1992). As we acknowledge our own efforts to understand history and the accomplishments of others, we begin to see how we are a part of that history as well. We start to realize that with knowledge comes the responsibility to act, as those we've just studied have done. We come to see that each of us, like a small quilt block depicting one part of a vision that includes all beings, can be joined together to create a more complex—but at the same time, more beautiful—expression of that vision.

Scientists on the Move

It used to annoy me in elementary school when we'd have projects assigned for homework and some of my peers would bring in their elaborate masterpieces. The part that exasperated me was the fact that their parents had done most of it for them. They knew it, the teacher knew it, and I knew it. That never happened in our home. My parents insisted that I do all of my own work. They wouldn't do it for me, and they wouldn't give me the answers. They wanted me to do my own thinking and my own creating. At the time it didn't seem fair, when many of my classmates were receiving so much assistance. I wanted intellectual welfare, and my parents refused to give it. What they did give me, however, was a seemingly endless supply of raw materials with which to find my own answers. They gave me an outdoor environment full of mud, sand, clay, open spaces, trees, grass, bushes, and water. They gave me scraps of wood and fabric, glue, cardboard, paint, and the freedom and tools to come up with my own answers. Above all else, they instilled in me the belief that I was fully capable of finding solutions to the problems laid before me.

Eight-year-old Rachel, who was in my class the year before, was helping me prepare the classroom for the new school year. We had taken on the task of peeling the paper off our old collection of crayons. To facilitate the process, we placed the crayons in a tub of water. Standing together, both of us with our hands in the water, I asked Rachel what she'd done all summer. She told me of her trip to Boston with her grandmother and of her fishing trip to San Diego. Rachel also proudly reported that she read several *Boxcar Children* books, one in just a day. Then she added, "And I did lots of studies on my own." When I asked her to elaborate, she explained that she picked topics, such as otters, and wrote about them. I asked, "Did you go to the library and get books about your studies?"

"No," she said, "I just asked a lot of people that might know and wrote it down."

I was delighted when this conversation with Rachel transpired. As a teacher I am always thrilled when I realize that my students have internalized the processes we have experienced in class. I was pleased the day Tyler came into the room with a map of the Underground Railroad. He had gone to the library with his mom the night before and independently looked up the Underground Railroad on the library computer, found the map in a book, and asked to make a copy for our study. I was equally happy when I realized Rachel had continued to conduct her own studies throughout the summer.

One of my goals for all of my students is to help them become lifelong learners. Whenever we carry out a class study, they are not only being exposed to the content, but are also becoming familiar with a process of learning that they can carry with them. As a result of our various studies throughout the year, Rachel knew what to do when she had a question about a subject. She was familiar with potential sources of information, and she knew what to do with the information when she received it.

Much of the curriculum I have described so far is related to class studies that evolve around a concept or theme. They are studies that often engage the entire class awhile and are then set aside for other work. Invariably we refer back to these studies from time to time, but they generally stand on their own. In addition to these more specific studies, there is other ongoing work that influences children like Rachel to pursue studies on their own. The ongoing work to which I am referring is in science.

I was delighted to discover a wonderful book several years back which takes the constructivist approach to science for young children. In *Young Child as Scientist,* Britain and Chaillé (1991) suggest that we help children pose questions about scientific phenomena, give them the materials with which to explore their questions, and then let them construct their own knowledge of their physical world. Influenced greatly by their ideas, we usually begin our science work with a simple question: How can I make something move? Available to the children are marbles, blocks, wooden ramps, metal trays, balls, corks, water, paper tubes, assorted washers and wire, and a variety of other odds and ends. On the first day of exploration, Leor constructed his own marble run and then checked out the work of his peers. He noticed that Anna and Kavita were having some difficulty with theirs. Apparently they were trying to make a marble roll down a ramp and funnel through a paper plate device at the bottom. Their problem was that the marble kept getting stuck on the edge of the plate. Leor offered his services. After making a few minor adjustments, he helped them complete a successful run with the marble. At the end of the science period, Leor recorded his experience in his science log (see Figure 23).

Over several months the children developed their scientific thinking through similar experiences. The structure of the inquiry was always the same, although the focus changed weekly. Each week we would begin with a focusing question which the entire class would determine. Some sample questions:

◆ How can I make something jump?
◆ How can I make a sound with something that moves?
◆ How can I make a chain reaction?
◆ How can I make something fly?
◆ How can I change the speed of something that moves?
◆ How can I make a unique pathway?
◆ How can I make something balance?
◆ How can I measure how long or short something is?
◆ How can I make something float in the air?

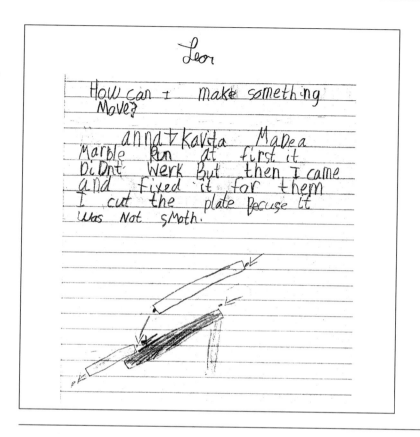

Leor

How can I make something Move?

anna + Kavita MaDe a Marble Ran at first it DiDnt Werk But then I came and Fixed it for them I cut the plate Becuse it Was Not sMoth.

Leor's explanation of how he helped Anna and Kavita with their marble-rolling chute.

Figure 23

Once the focusing question was determined, the children went to work on it.

For the next forty-five minutes to an hour, they would set up their own experiments using the available equipment and materials. The advantage of the focusing question was that it helped them stay concentrated on a specific idea. Without it their activity turned into free play. Often during this period I would check in with each group and ask them how what they were doing related to the focusing question. For example, one day the focusing question concerned how to make something float in the air. When I noticed Ashley and Margaret spending a lot of time on an egg carton apparatus, I asked them what their work had to do with floating. After making a small adjustment, they gave me a demonstration. Margaret recorded their work in her log (see Figure 24).

I learned early on that the emphasis needed to be on observing and recording what was actually happening. This took time and practice for the children. During one day's work, Danielle noticed that rubbing a piece of wood with

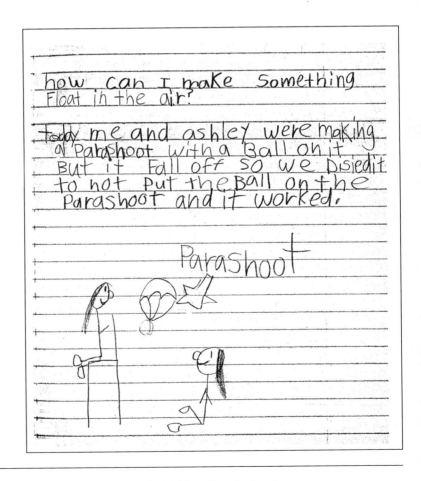

Figure 24   Margaret's report on making things float in the air.

sandpaper not only made the wood smooth but also produced heat. During a follow-up discussion, one child said that was friction. The child had heard the term but couldn't explain what it was. We made a strong effort to try to explain what we observed (e.g., heat made when two objects were rubbed together) rather than giving the phenomenon an abstract label.

The week after Danielle's discovery, we decided to use what she had noticed as part of our focusing question: How many different ways can I make heat with something that moves? Children came up with a variety of methods for recording their data. Leor made a list of what he used and indicated on the margin whether it made heat or not. Narcissa indicated her findings through drawings (Figure 25). When this day's explorations were over, we wondered why

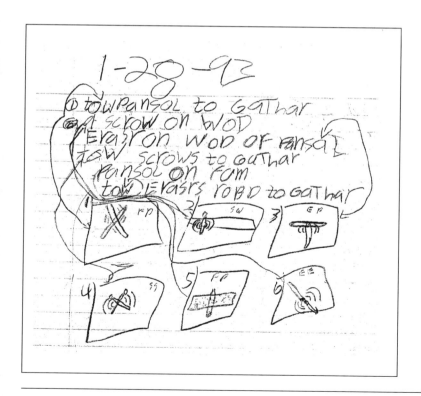

Narcissa's findings for her heat-making experiments.

Figure 25

some objects created heat when rubbed together and some didn't. We found our next focusing question: How are things that make heat different from things that don't?

Initially this concept was difficult for many of the children to grasp, but after applying it to concrete experiences they were able to understand it. Leor was one of the first to realize that a clue to the puzzle had to do with textures. The children who were able to describe their actions through words or pictures were the most successful. Danielle's log entry (Figure 26) not only showed what she and others did but also included what she learned from it. Our follow-up discus-

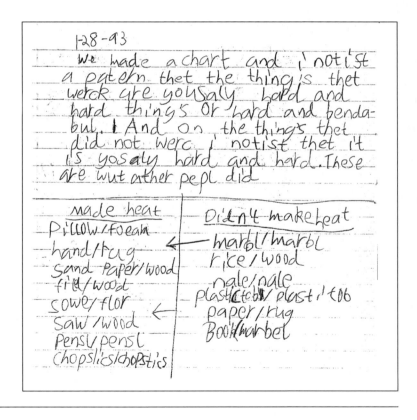

Figure 26   Danielle's science-log entry on objects that make heat when rubbed together.

sion was rich with discovery but also was not without moments of humor. Leor reported that he had tried rubbing two marbles together and found they created heat. When he noticed others had tried the same experiment with opposite results, he tried it again. He approached me at the end of the day and said, "I want to change what I said about the marbles. It didn't work. I must have had a hot marble the first time."

Over time the children became more adept both at thinking of questions that encouraged rich exploration and at describing their work. I was always amazed at the innovative ways they would approach a problem. One of the most fascinating moments was the day Kevin and Nick used clear plastic tubes, water, marbles, and corks to figure out how to change the speed of something that moves. They spent an entire afternoon observing the variable speed of a marble and water inside a corked tube. Specifically, they noticed that the speed of the marble changed when it hit an air bubble. Kevin summarized their work in his log, summarized in Figure 27.

It was also interesting to see how different children approached the same question. On the day we posed the question "How can I make something balance?", there was a variety of responses. Narcissa made a scale from cups, yarn, and a plastic tray. She put marbles in each cup to make them balance. Kevin and Leor devised a balance using a hanger, small plastic cups, rice, and string. They held the cardboard part of the hanger in their mouths with the rest of it attached to the rest of the hanger (see Figure 28). Nick took a completely different approach and made his balance with wood and nails. It was exciting and encouraging to see the children develop confidence in their own thinking. As our weeks of scientific inquiry accumulated, they devised more and more ways to find answers to questions. It was fascinating to see how they drew other aspects of classroom life into responses to the focusing questions. Some children, like Nick, frequently turned to the woodworking equipment. Others consistently chose blocks to explore chain reactions, sounds, pathways, speed of objects, and balance. There were yet other children who often turned their science to art. On the day the class

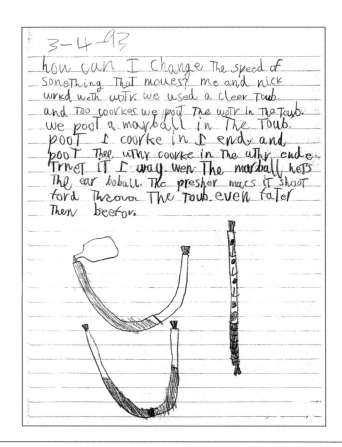

Figure 27   Kevin's report on his and Nick's experiment on changing the speed of a
moving object. His text reads: "How can I change the speed of something
that moves? Me and Nick worked with water. We used a clear tube and
two corks. We put the water in the tube. We put a marble in the tube.
Put 1 cork in 1 end and put the other cork in the other end. Turned it
one way. When the marble hits the air bubble the pressure makes it
shoot forward through the tube even faster than before."

posed the question "How can I make a sound with something
that moves?", most of the class ended up making their own
version of a rain stick—a device of African origin that consists
of a long, hollow stick sealed off at both ends. Inside the

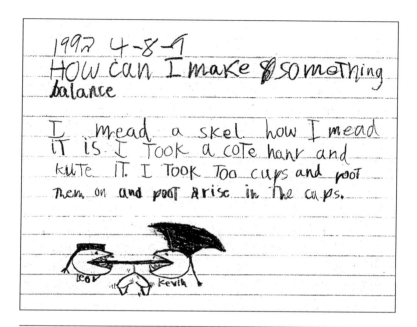

Kevin's report on the scale he made with Leor. His text reads: "How can I make something balance. I made a scale. How I made it is I took a coat hanger and cut it. I took two cups and put them on and put rice in the cups."

Figure 28

stick, which in its natural state has small spines inside, seeds are shifted from one end to the other. As the seeds hit the spines, it sounds like rain. When the children made these they used long cardboard tubes with nails hammered in the sides, beans, and lots of tape to contain the beans.

I noticed that some of the children also brought their own interests and experiences to their work. On the same day that we explored sounds and things that move, Susan, Nick, and Kjirsten set up an experiment using washers, bolts, and wire. They tested the pitch of each different-sized washer and even devised a system for recording their findings. This two-week experiment was summarized by Susan's log entry in Figure 29. Clearly she brought her own passion and interest in music to this work, as well as her sense of humor.

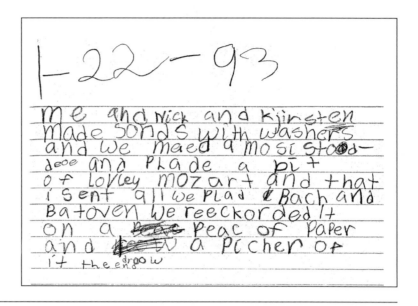

Figure 29   Susan's report on making music with washers. The text reads: "Me and Nick
              and Kjirsten made sounds with washers and we made a music studio and
              played a bit of lovely Mozart and that isn't all. We played Bach and Beethoven.
              We recorded it on a piece of paper and drew a picture of it. The end."

     In addition to developing as scientists, the children grew
as observers. This was evident in their actual work and also in
the way they reported what they did. Many of the children
came to write more. Others, like Braden, relied on their drawing abilities to communicate what occurred. In Braden's log
entry, shown in Figure 30, he explains what his group did one
day. But his picture, almost cartoon-like, reveals the lively dialogue that took place as he and his friends tried to make a
washer "float" across the air with a magnet. As our work with
scientific inquiry developed, the children learned to apply their
abilities to write and draw and think together. This, in turn,
helped to extend their scientific knowledge. It was this process
of combining multiple skills and disciplines that made the
work significant. By drawing on what they already knew and
putting it together with a new problem or situation, they came

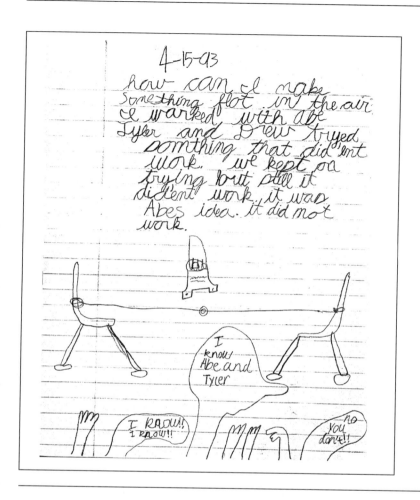

Braden's report on working with Abe, Drew, and Tyler to make something float through the air.

Figure 30

to realize their strength as learners. This process was exciting
for all of us because new discoveries appeared each week. It
didn't matter what the focusing question was or what materials
were being used. The process always revealed similar results.
Although our work was usually restricted to physical science,
we did use other materials and, on occasion, worked with
solutions and mixtures.

When the warm spring afternoons arrived, we moved our scientific work outside. We gathered our bubble equipment—large metal trays, plastic hoops, funnels, tubes, and an assortment of other paraphernalia—and headed for the basketball court outside our classroom. Working in small groups, the children organized their equipment and mixed their bubble solutions. They used dish soap, corn syrup, and various quantities of water. Before long, one group produced an array of tiny bubbles blown through pieces of plastic screen. Alongside them another group of children was making huge five-foot bubbles by pulling a hoop rapidly off the tray. The bubbles were as varied as the children who produced them.

The work with bubbles, like the previous explorations with physical science, offered the children opportunities to apply their knowledge in new ways. When we worked with bubble solutions, the initial experimentation was mostly play. In a loosely structured way, the children tried out several ways to make bubbles. They compared bubbles made with skinny tubes and juice cans. They used the large plastic rings for huge bubbles and tried to produce the same results with an apparatus made of yarn and plastic straws. They made "cakes" out of bubbles. They found ways to make bubbles they could carry around on the palms of their hands. As with previous work, they recorded their results in their science logs. When bubbles were made available on repeated occasions, the children also came up with new problems they wanted to solve, based on their previous experimentation. One afternoon they decided on these two challenges:

◆ How can I make gigantic bubbles?
◆ How can I make a bubble inside of another bubble?

It was fascinating to see how they applied their previous experiences to the bubbles. The opportunity to revisit the same materials and processes on consecutive weeks gave the children time to develop a history with their work. They got to know bubbles through direct experiences, and they also had time in between to think about bubbles. The accumulation of experiences and time for reflection not only increased the children's ability to ask questions and think of ways to find the answers; it also helped them become more proficient at recording their results.

I observed other influences of the science work in the children's writing and use of language. One day we had experimented with cornstarch, water, and food coloring. Following this experience, Jacob wrote in his daily writing book, "The cornstarch gave me a bad feeling like if someone took a piece of chalk and pushed it down a chalkboard and [made] a squeaky sound. And one was gooey and one was like cement." Several weeks later, Brandon and Jacob were sitting together at the computer talking about the screeching sounds of humpback whales. Jacob was stuck on the ending for his piece about whales, and Brandon was trying to help. Brandon suddenly remembered the entry that Jacob had shared from his daily writing book on a previous day. Brandon said, "You know that poem [the entry about the cornstarch]? You could use that here in your story." Jacob hesitated and Brandon added, "But it's okay. It's your own words." He was helping Jacob draw a connection between his two pieces of writing and at the same time acknowledging that Jacob was the writer with the final say about the direction his work should go. This incident not only gave me a glimpse of the children's growing understanding of a writer's process, but it also indicated the increased ways in which their independent inquiries with science, mathematics, blocks, and other projects influenced their thinking.

A picture stays in my mind of the day I watched a group of children experimenting with colored markers, coffee filters, assorted paper strips, and water. They would draw colored dots on the strips and then dip them in the water. They tested the absorbency of the various papers as well as observed how the different colors separated when they became wet. Each child had his or her own standard of evaluation. I chuckled as I watched Shannon eliminate one strip of paper and say, "This paper won't suck up very good!" As they continued their testing, they soon realized that the coffee filters were the most successful for absorbency. Through experimentation, the children created many elaborate designs by drawing on the filters and then dipping the filters in water.

Reflecting on this work, I can see now that the children's minds were much like the coffee filters brightly decorated with markers. As they were dipped in the waters of scientific inquiry, new thoughts were soaked up and transformed. Each design was unique, due to its color combinations and length of time in the water. Our days of learning together were no less varied, for each one contained the same element of potential for beauty, surprise, and wonder. It happened because children were given the resources to uncover exciting possibilities—and also the belief in themselves that they were capable of carrying out such work.

Enabling children to feel this way about themselves as learners is one of the greatest tasks that lies before us as teachers. Whether our students are composing a poem, trying to understand the movement of a marble through a maze of blocks, or using their small hands to create a miniature hotel for their stuffed animals, it is our responsibility to give them everything possible to further their work. We do this by giving them the materials and tools they need to pursue answers to their questions. We do it by offering them a supportive environment in which to make their inquiries. And we do it through our own efforts to enrich both our inner and outer lives, to become more whole.

Making a Teaching Life

*During my adolescent summers, I was sent off to a girls' camp in
northern Minnesota. It was there that I began to understand the
importance of cultivating my inner life. Walking along dirt pathways
among the tall pines, hearing the waves gently lapping against the
docks, and developing friendships with others who wondered about
some of life's same questions awakened a desire in me to live my life
as fully and deeply as possible. During my summers beside the lake, I
became a sailor and developed another significant relationship—with
the water and the wind. Each time I ventured out in a boat I felt
engaged in a dance with the essence of nature itself. I loved being the
connecting link between the wind, the water, and my sailing craft.
When my friends and I would take a boat out, particularly on days
when the lake was covered with whitecaps, we learned to push the
edge of our skill as sailors. We would highside the boat to the point
where the upper bilge was completely out of the water. Then one of us
would stand on it and ride along, leaning out as far as we could until
we had to come about. As we did this we checked ourselves and our
position on the edge by shouting at each other, "Do you have it?"*

*When I think of those times, our bodies drenched with water
and our hearts soaked with a newfound sense of power and possibility,
I remember also the poem that so perfectly described how I felt about
those days:*

> *With all the powers of your body concentrated in the hand on
> the tiller,*
> *All the powers of your mind concentrated on the goal beyond
> the horizon,*

You laugh as the salt spray catches your face in the second of rest
Before a new wave—
Sharing the happy freedom of the moment with those who share
    your responsibility.
So—in the self-forgetfulness of concentrated attention—
    the door opens for you into a pure living intimacy,
A shared, timeless happiness,
Conveyed by a smile,
A wave of the hand.

>   *Thanks to those who have taught me this. Thanks to the days*
>   *which have taught me this.*

>   —Dag Hammarskjöld
>   *Markings* (1966)

The days when I sailed and pushed the edge provided some of the most significant lessons of my life. From those experiences I learned that life along the edge certainly has its possibilities if we dare to travel there. Terry Tempest Williams (1994) writes that "we must undress, expose, and embrace our authentic selves . . . We must journey out, so that we might journey in." When we learn more about who we are along the edge, we discover endless treasures and surprises that can only be found by those who are willing to take risks. I see this every day with my students. Those who aren't afraid to paint that extra splash of color are the ones who create the most wonderful artwork. The authors who dare to reveal the tiniest details of their lives receive the most frequent requests for more stories from their audience. The young scientist who takes the chance that her precarious tower might fall is the one who learns the most about balance.

From my own experience I have realized that as human beings we only feel secure in traveling along that edge when we know we have a safe sanctuary to which to return. In my youth, my friends and I knew we could take our chances while sailing because there was always someone following our adventures from the dock, prepared to come and rescue us if necessary. We also knew that unless we were guilty of some sort of gross misconduct, we would not be punished for our actions. We knew that if we stayed within the accepted safety guidelines and used good judgment, we were free to stretch ourselves and the limits of our abilities. We had teachers who trusted us and gave us that freedom. As my skills as a sailor developed, my teachers began to entrust me with more and more responsibility. I learned to trust my own instincts and make the right decisions. My increasing awareness of the natural world also made me realize in a new way that something existed—much greater than myself—which held all of life together. I began to understand that I was a part of the great inbreathing and outbreathing of life and that I must trust that it would provide me with whatever I need.

Learning to travel the edge has become a daily practice in my life. It prevails in my work as a teacher, and particularly as the director of a handmade school. It has given me faith in myself to be a risk taker and know that even though I might falter at times, whatever happens will contain an element of goodness. This practice is present in everything I do, both in and outside of school. It has taught me to have fun and honor the adventurer in myself, the one who must walk often among trees and explore desert canyons. At the same time, this practice has reminded me to bring that sense of humor and adventure into my classroom each day, to bring my students a bit of the wildness I've encountered in my wanderings.

My practice of pushing the edge has also made me recognize the necessity we all have for self-expression. Certainly teaching is a form of self-expression for many of us in the classroom. As I grow in experience and age, I see that my personal expression must come in a variety of other ways, too—through words, movement, fibers, colors and textures, and making things with my hands. Knowing this has opened my eyes to the collection of young artists before me who have their own assortment of expressive needs and desires. Recognizing and honoring the artist in myself has enabled me to do the same for the youthful artists who surround me each day. It has made me see that when our lives move along the edge of possibility, we have more ideas and choices available to us, both as artists and adventurers.

As a teacher I have realized that there are times when I need to slow down and give myself quiet moments for reflection, for not only the adventurer and the artist must be honored, but also the one who longs for solitude. I have found it essential to build opportunities for silence, meditation, and contemplation into each day. Our best ideas come when we have quiet moments to consider thoughts, questions, and possibilities. Out of silence and time spent listening to our inner voice emerges intuition.

Listening to my inner voice has been the single most important factor in my continued practice as a teacher. It is what guides me in my decisions each day regarding how I will conduct my classroom and determine what the curriculum will be. It is what reminds me to choose a certain book for a class study or abandon the planned activity for an hour of sketching on a beautiful morning. Intuition is a built-in mentor who, when I am quiet enough to pay attention, shows me what is next. The more I am able to listen, the stronger the voice of intuition becomes.

One important way in which I've learned to pay closer attention to intuition is by being a better observer of my students. Although it is difficult, I've found it to be one of the most valuable parts of my practice. When I take more time to observe, I can see more clearly the many wonderful interactions and choices transpiring. It is during these moments that I have my clearest understandings of what it means to make school by hand.

Just recently we were in the midst of our Friday afternoon projects. There were a few rare minutes when nobody needed me to thread the sewing machine, attend to the computer, or retrieve some desired material from the top of the art shelf. That moment brought a sense of clarity I cannot forget. It brought an awareness of the continuity of my teaching life and the steady flow of learning that keeps going along when we don't obstruct its path.

As I looked around the room at the children, I could see them all seriously at work on whatever they considered important. Each of them was undertaking a project that was pleasurable, interesting, and leading toward further discovery. Everything going on around me seemed directly connected to some aspect of what had come before—either in the current school year or even further back in previous years. I noticed Jana on the floor with Julie, our student teacher, sewing a yellow corduroy pillow, and I remembered helping Jana's older brother Robert make *his* pillow not so long ago. Close by, Mya was helping me sort out the flyers for the monthly book orders. She noticed one of the books available and said, "Look, Mary!" It was a book on Indian chiefs—a new resource for our current study of Native Americans. At the same table Jake and Arianna were engrossed in making miniature tepees for Jake's individual study of the Lakota Sioux. Jake had thought of the idea for our study and wanted to share the technique with anyone who was interested. On the table behind Jake and Arianna, four girls were working on a group project called "Sally's Haunted Hotel." It was a wooden construction for one girl's stuffed mouse that was a continuation of a paper house they'd worked on for several months in their first grade class the year before. The "hotel" was equipped with a variety of furnishings to go along with the Halloween theme.

While I sat at the table helping Mya with her sorting, J. D. approached me and said, "Hey, Mary, I made a lice game." Needless to say, we'd had those pesky visitors in our class again, and J. D. had the experience on his mind (fortunately, no longer in his hair!). He had created his game using card-sized pieces of wood with a green triangle and the word *lice* on one side, and a number and some small black dots on the other side. The dots on the high numbered cards were lice and the low ones were nits. Each player took two cards and then added up the total of the numbers on the back. Whoever had the highest total won the game. I was delighted with his game, not only from a humorous standpoint, but also with the thinking that had been so quickly and cleverly applied. J. D. had not only used a theme that was prevalent in our room, but he had also incorporated many of the skills he'd learned the previous year as a first-grade maker of math games.

J. D.'s lice game reminded me of a scene the day before when lice had also taken a place in the curriculum. He and Joelle, both just returned from a day away from school with their second round of lice, were each at a computer composing a text about lice. J. D.'s became a flap book, and Joelle wrote a poem which eventually ended up in our class poetry collection (Figure 31).

LICE

Lice, oh Lice,
Will you stop coming?
I hate you and so does my mom.
And I want to go back to school.
Why, oh, why do you like my head?
And every time you come
My mom has to clean my bed.
I got to chew some bubble gum.
And I taught myself how to blow bubbles.
My mother is superstitious.
She believes I got lice today
Because yesterday
She put the lice shampoo away
And returned the lice books to the library.

--Joelle

Figure 31   Joelle's poem on the return of the lice.

J. D.'s lice game and the writing of the two children were indications once again of how life becomes curriculum when we leave a space for it. As I looked around at my students busily engaged in their current passions, I could see how committed they were to learning. I felt the pulse of life in our classroom, in our school. For what was happening and continues to happen each day is a process of composing that includes an environment, learning events that hold meaning to the people who inhabit that environment, and the people themselves who happen to care a great deal about each other and what they do together. Each moment, each day, each school year, is held together by this common element of caring. We take whomever is present, open our eyes to what surrounds us in the world, and busy ourselves with the task of asking what is important. We answer that question through what we talk about, what we write, and who we invite into our community through story, song, or painting. We absorb whatever comes to our door and make it our own. Each day is a new act of creating, like painting on a fresh blank canvas, filled with great anticipation for what might appear on it. It is ongoing, unpredictable, exhilarating—and as full of possibility as the world that envelopes us. As artists, adventurers, and thinkers we embrace each moment, expecting it to reveal a bit more understanding of what it means to be on this human journey together.

In addition to keeping our eyes wide open to what goes on in the classroom, we need to approach the rest of our lives with the same wide-awakeness. Often what we need for growth and greater understanding as teachers comes in unexpected situations. Sometimes what apparently pulls us away from our work as teachers often brings us back with new insight.

As I mentioned earlier, this book began the same summer I sewed a quilt for my friend's unborn baby. Caitlin Elizabeth was born the day after Christmas, and I was fortunate enough to be present for her birth. Caitlin and I quickly became friends, and it was a wonderful experience to hold her wrapped in the quilt I had sewn for her. My devotion to my writing diminished in the months that followed as my devotion to her increased. More than writing about school, I seemed to need the quiet joy I experienced in the late afternoons when she and her mom and I would sit outside and blow bubbles together. I was always fascinated by the way she used her hands to pop the bubbles, reach for my silver earrings, or point to the night sky.

When Caitlin was ten-and-a-half months old, she was diagnosed with cancer. My writing was set aside even more as I devoted any extra time I had to helping out with her treatment and care. Sometimes I just went to her house to play; and other times when she was in the hospital, I'd walk her up and down the hallways in her stroller, IV tubes attached. Wherever we were, regardless of how sick she was, she nearly always had a smile. We grew to be dear friends.

A few weeks after her second birthday, Caitlin passed away. She remained strong and remarkably courageous until the very end. All along I had looked forward to the day when I would be her second-grade teacher. Knowing that this would never happen caused me great sadness. Then I realized that I had, indeed, been her teacher—and she had been mine. I had read her Spot books and played funny games with her. One memorable evening, while out for a neighborhood stroll, I taught her the word "moon." She, in turn, taught me to slow down and pay attention to the details of seemingly insignificant moments. She reminded me to keep my eyes open to the color of the sunset, the delicacy of a flower petal, the song of a bird. As she used her hands to communicate what she couldn't say in words, she instilled in me a realization that I must continue to use both my words and my hands as much as I can, especially in my work as a teacher.

Although it may appear on the surface that my work with words was interrupted by Caitlin's short life, I believe my time with her was an important teaching I needed to receive. The insights I gained, particularly regarding unconditional love, have significantly altered the way I approach everything, especially in the classroom. I have learned from her to savor every moment and not take anything for granted. I've become more aware of the need to celebrate the small daily accomplishments that happen with children and not just wait for the more obvious ones. I've been inspired to write about what I think and know, in hope that the kind of love and joy I knew as her teacher can be available to others.

My brief encounter with the child for whom I stitched the baby quilt three summers ago brought to light the profound impact we can have on each other's lives when we open ourselves to experiences that sometimes involve risk. There are times when life draws us into situations that demand more of us than we sometimes care to give. If we hold back we remain safe, but we miss out on a deeper kind of knowing. We may experience suffering and find ourselves stretched beyond what we thought were our limits, but we will also come to know unimaginable joys. As teachers and makers of schools, we owe these possibilities to ourselves— as well as to each child who crosses our path.

References

Bemelmans, Ludwig. 1939. *Madeline.* New York: Viking.

Bunting, Eve. 1990. *The Wall.* New York: Houghton Mifflin.

Burnett, Frances Hodgson. 1987. *The Secret Garden.* Boston: David R. Godine.

Castle, Kathryn. 1990. "Children's Invented Games." *Childhood Education* 67: 82–85.

Cech, John. 1991. *My Grandmother's Journey.* New York: Bradbury.

Chaillé, Christine, and Lori Britain. 1991. *The Young Child as Scientist.* New York: HarperCollins.

D'Aulaire, Ingri, and Edgar Parin d'Aulaire. 1939. *Abraham Lincoln.* New York: Doubleday.

Derman-Sparks, Louise, and the A.B.C. Task Force. 1989. *Anti-Bias Curriculum: Tools for Empowering Young Children.* Washington, D. C.: National Association for the Education of Young Children.

Dewey, John. [1913] 1970. *Interest and Effort in Education.* Reprint, New York: Augustus M. Kelley.

Dewey, John, and Evelyn Dewey. 1915. *Schools of To-morrow.* New York: E. P. Dutton.

Duckworth, Eleanor. 1987. *"The Having of Wonderful Ideas" and Other Essays on Teaching and Learning*. New York: Teachers College Press.

Frasier, Debra. 1991. *On the Day You Were Born*. San Diego: Harcourt Brace Jovanovich.

Geisel, Theodore Seuss. 1957. *The Cat in the Hat*. Boston: Houghton Mifflin.

—. 1974. *How the Grinch Stole Christmas*. New York: Random House.

—. 1971. *The Lorax*. New York: Random House.

Glover, Mary, and Linda Sheppard. 1989. *Not on Your Own: The Power of Learning Together*. Richmond Hill, Ontario: Scholastic-TAB.

Hamilton, Virginia. 1985. *The People Could Fly*. New York: Alfred A. Knopf.

Hammarskjöld, Dag. 1966. *Markings*. New York: Alfred A. Knopf.

Jeffers, Susan. 1991. *Brother Eagle, Sister Sky: A Message from Chief Seattle*. New York: Dial.

Mayeroff, Milton. 1971. *On Caring*. New York: Harper and Row.

McLerran, Alice. 1991. *Roxaboxen*. New York: William Morrow and Company.

Mearns, Hughes. [1929] 1958. *Creative Power: The Education of Youth in the Creative Arts*. Reprint, New York: Dover.

Paterson, Katherine. 1990. "Heart in Hiding." In *Worlds of Childhood: The Art and Craft of Writing for Children*, edited by William Zinsser. Boston: Houghton Mifflin.

Pete, Bill. 1970. *The Wump World*. New York: Houghton Mifflin.

Peterson, Ralph. 1992. *Life in a Crowded Place: Making a Learning Community.* Portsmouth, New Hampshire: Heinemann.

Rice, Paul, and Peter Mayle. 1981. *As Dead as a Dodo.* Boston: David R. Godine.

Turner, Ann. 1987. *Nettie's Trip South.* New York: Scholastic.

Van Allsburg, Chris. 1981. *Jumanji.* New York: Houghton Mifflin.

Welty, Eudora. 1983. *One Writer's Beginnings.* Cambridge, Massachusetts: Harvard University Press.

Williams, Terry Tempest. 1994. *An Unspoken Hunger.* New York: Pantheon.

Winter, Jonah. 1991. *Diego.* Illustrated by Jeanette Winter. New York: Alfred A. Knopf.

Recommended Readings

Chaillé, Christine, and Lori Britain. 1991. *The Young Child as Scientist.* New York: HarperCollins.

This small volume has revolutionized my thinking and practice in science education. It philosophically and theoretically supports what I believe is appropriate for young children's acquisition of knowledge about their physical world.

Fletcher, Ralph. 1993. *What a Writer Needs.* Portsmouth, New Hampshire: Heinemann.

When I feel like giving up on being a writer, all I have to do is pick up this book and somehow it manages to pull me back into the heart of why I write—and why I must write.

Glover, Mary Kenner. 1993. *Two Years: A Teacher's Memoir.* Portsmouth, New Hampshire: Heinemann.

A description of the author's two years with the same class. This book offers another in-depth view of life in a handmade school.

Goldberg, Natalie. 1993. *Long Quiet Highway.* New York: Bantam.

Sometimes we view our professional lives as separate from our spiritual lives. In this book the author shows us a way to "wake up" and see how the two can actually be one if we learn to live our lives as our spiritual practice.

Heard, Georgia. 1989. *For the Good of the Earth and Sun: Teaching Poetry*. Portsmouth, NH: Heinemann.

The best book I know on teaching poetry to children. It is a wonderful blend of sensitive reflections on poetry and practical know-how for teaching poetry in the classroom.

_____ . 1995. *Writing toward Home: Tales and Lessons to Find Your Way*. Portsmouth, NH: Heinemann.

An inspiring collection of vignettes and suggestions for writers who wish to make their voices stronger and more clear. This book helps writers slow down and see the poetry and stories that accompany us through our lives.

Paley, Vivian. 1992. *You Can't Say You Can't Play*. Cambridge, Massachusetts: Harvard University Press.

An examination of social dynamics between young children, in particular the issue of inclusion and exclusion. This book has significantly influenced and improved the play of children at my school.

_____. 1995. *Kwanzaa and Me: A Teacher's Story*. Cambridge, Massachusetts: Harvard University Press.

A thought-provoking book which encourages dialogue between parents and teachers regarding racial issues in the classroom. The author emphasizes the importance of the classroom teacher's role in improving interracial relationships.

Peterson, Ralph. 1992. *Life in a Crowded Place: Making a Learning Community*. Portsmouth, NH: Heinemann.

An important philosophical examination of what goes into establishing classroom communities and what we can do to further holistic thinking in our daily teaching practices.

Sarton, May. 1973. *Journal of a Solitude*. New York: Norton.

In a teacher's busy life, surrounded all day long by people, it's a good idea to remember to replenish ourselves with moments of solitude.

Welty, Eudora. 1983. *One Writer's Beginnings.* Cambridge, Massachusetts: Harvard University Press.

A remarkable examination of one writer's early life and how it influenced her later career. Through reading about one person's childhood, we can gather insights about our own.

Williams, Terry Tempest. 1994. *An Unspoken Hunger.* New York: Pantheon.

Intimacy with our natural world and its effect on our intimacy with our deeper selves is a theme of this book. Although not directly addressing teaching, Williams' book is a valuable text for anyone wanting to be more aware of themselves and those whose lives they touch.

Author

PHOTO: JOHN LAMAR

Mary Kenner Glover was born and raised in a rural Nebraska community. She has lived and worked in Arizona since the early 1970s. Seeking an alternative educational setting for her two young daughters, she co-founded Awakening Seed School in Tempe, Arizona, in 1977, where she is currently the director and second-grade teacher. She completed her master of arts degree in elementary education at Arizona State University in 1988. She has authored *Charlie's Ticket to Literacy, Two Years: A Teacher's Memoir*, and co-authored *Not on Your Own: The Power of Learning Together*. In addition to her work as a teacher and educational consultant, she is a poet and an artist. She lives in Tempe, Arizona, with her husband and youngest daughter.

◆

This book's interior and cover were typeset in Goudy, Optima, and Addled by Doug Burnett. The book was printed on 60 lb. Williamsburg by Versa Press.